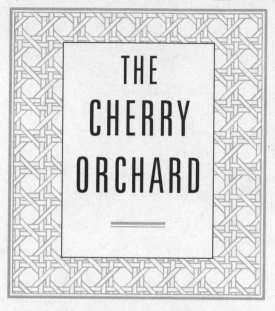

THE
CHERRY
ORCHARD

ALSO BY LAURENCE SENELICK

The Seagull (translator)

Three Sisters (translator)

The Complete Plays: Anton Chekhov (translator and editor)

Russian Dramatic Theory from Pushkin to the Symbolists

The Chekhov Theatre: A Century of the Plays in Performance

Russian Satiric Comedy (translator)

Gordon Craig's Moscow Hamlet

Serf Actor: The Life and Art of Mikhail Shchepkin

National Theatre in Northern and Eastern Europe (editor)

Historical Dictionary of Russian Theater

THE
CHERRY
ORCHARD

ANTON CHEKHOV

Translated by

LAURENCE SENELICK

W. W. NORTON & COMPANY

NEW YORK   LONDON

For information about permission to reproduce
selections from this book, write to Permissions,
W. W. Norton & Company, Inc.,
500 Fifth Avenue, New York, NY 10110

For information about special discounts for bulk
purchases, please contact W. W. Norton Special Sales
at specialsales@wwnorton.com or 800-233-4830

Manufacturing by Courier Westford
Book design by JAM Design
Production manager: Devon Zahn

Library of Congress Cataloging-in-Publication Data

Chekhov, Anton Pavlovich, 1860–1904.
[Vishnevyi sad. English]
The cherry orchard / Anton Chekhov ; translated
by Laurence Senelick. — 1st ed.
p. cm.
Includes bibliographical references.
ISBN 978-0-393-33816-4 (pbk.)
I. Senelick, Laurence. II. Title.
PG3456.V5S38 2010
891.72'3—dc22

2010018094

W. W. Norton & Company, Inc.
500 Fifth Avenue, New York, N.Y. 10110
www.wwnorton.com

W. W. Norton & Company Ltd.
Castle House, 75/76 Wells Street, London W1T 3QT

1 2 3 4 5 6 7 8 9 0

This edition is dedicated to the cast and
crew of the Agassiz Theatre production
at Harvard University.

CONTENTS

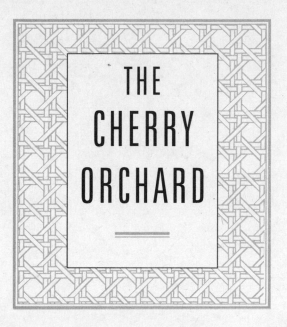

THE
CHERRY
ORCHARD

ANTON CHEKHOV'S BRIEF LIFE

Anton Pavlovich Chekhov was born in the town of Taganrog on the sea of Azov in southern Russia on January 17, 1860,[1] the third of six children, five boys and a girl. He might have been born a serf, as his father, Pavel Yegorovich, had, for the Emancipation came only in 1861; but his grandfather, a capable and energetic estate manager named Yegor Chekh, had prospered so well that in 1841 he had purchased his freedom along with his family's. Anton's mother, Yevgeniya Morozova, was the orphaned daughter of a cloth merchant and a subservient spouse to her despotic husband. To their children, she imparted a sensibility he lacked: Chekhov would later say, somewhat unfairly, that they inherited their talent from their father and their soul from their mother.[2]

The talent was displayed in church. Beyond running a small grocery store where his sons served long hours—"In my childhood, there was no childhood," Anton was later to report[3]—Pavel Chekhov had a taste for the outward trappings of religion. This was satisfied by unfailing observance of the rites of the Eastern Orthodox Church, daily family worship, and, especially, liturgical music. He enrolled his sons in a choir that he founded and conducted, and he aspired to be a pillar of the community.

Taganrog, its once-prosperous port now silted up and neglected, had a population that exceeded fifty thousand during Chekhov's boyhood. Its residents included wealthy Greek families, the ship-building interests, and a large number of Jews, Tatars, and Armenians. The town benefited from such public amenities of the tsarist civil administration as a pretentious-looking *gymnasium*, which the Chekhov boys attended, for one of Pavel's aims was to procure his children the level of education needed for entry into the professions. The upward mobility of the Chekhov generations is reflected in the character of Lopakhin in *The Cherry Orchard*, a self-made millionaire whose ancestors had been serfs on the estate he succeeds in purchasing. Chekhov's father, born a serf, had risen from *meshchanin*, or petty bourgeois,[4] to be the member of a merchant guild; and Chekhov himself, as a physician and writer, became influential on the national scene. He was a model of the *raznochinets*, or person of no settled rank, who began to dominate Russian society in the latter half of the nineteenth century.

To impede mass advancement, the tsarist curriculum laid great stress on Greek and Latin. One recalls the schoolmaster Kulygin in *Three Sisters* chuckling over the fate of a classmate who missed promotion because he could not master the *ut consecutivum* construction. Schoolmasters are usually portrayed by Chekhov as narrow-minded, obsequious, and unimaginative, no doubt the result of his own observations as he studied the classics, German, Russian, and, for a brief time, French. His best subject was Scripture. School days were lightened by the fairy tales of his nanny, the picaresque reminiscences of his mother, vacations spent on the estate his grandfather managed, fishing, swimming, and, later, visits to the theater.

As a boy, Chekhov was stage-struck. Although it was against school regulations, he and his classmates, often in false whiskers and dark glasses, frequented the gallery of the active and imposing Taganrog Playhouse. He was also the star performer in domestic theatricals, playing comic roles such as the Mayor in *The Inspector* and the scrivener Chuprun in the Ukrainian folk opera *The Military Magician*. While still at school, he wrote a drama called *Without Patrimony* and a vaudeville (a farce with songs) called *The Hen Has Good Reason to Cluck*. Later, while a medical student, he tried to revise them, even as he completed another farce, *The Cleanshaven Secretary with the Pistol*, which his younger brother Mikhail recalls as being very funny. Never submitted to the government censorship office, which passed plays or forbade them from performance, it is now lost.

By 1876 Pavel Chekhov had so mismanaged his business that, fearing imprisonment for debt, he stole off to the next town, where he took the train to Moscow. There his two elder sons, Aleksandr and Nikolay, were pursuing their studies. He had already stopped paying his dues to the merchant guild and had reverted to the status of *meshchanin*. Whether Anton suffered a psychic trauma at this loss of caste, as had the young Henrik Ibsen when *his* father went bankrupt, is matter for speculation. Certainly, the repercussions felt at the sale of the home left their trace on many of his plays, including *Platonov* and *The Cherry Orchard*. Dispos-

sessed of home and furniture, his mother and the three young-
est children also departed for Moscow, abandoning Anton in a
house now owned by a friend of his father's. He had to support
himself by tutoring during the three years before he graduated.
He did not rejoin his family until Easter 1877, his fare paid by his
university-student brother Aleksandr. This first visit to Moscow
and its theaters set standards by which he henceforth judged the
quality of life in the provinces. Suddenly, Taganrog began to look
provincial.

Just before Anton Chekhov left Taganrog for good, a public
library opened. This enabled him to read classics such as *Don
Quixote* and *Hamlet*, a work he was to cite recurrently, and, like
any Victorian schoolboy, *Uncle Tom's Cabin* and the adventure
stories of Thomas Mayne Reid. Heavier reading included philo-
sophic works that enjoyed a high reputation at the time, such as
Thomas Henry Buckle's positivist and skeptical survey of Euro-
pean culture, *The History of Civilization in England.* Later in life,
Chekhov took a wry view of this omnivorous autodidacticism, and
had the clumsy bookkeeper Yepikhodov in *The Cherry Orchard*
allude to Buckle's works as a token of self-improvement.

It was at this time that Chekhov began writing prose, sending
comic pieces to Aleksandr in Moscow in the hope that they would
be accepted by the numerous comic journals that had sprung up
in the capitals. He made friends with actors, hung around back-
stage, and learned how to make up his face. Two of his school fel-
lows did enter the profession: Aleksandr Vishnevsky, who would
become a charter member of the Moscow Art Theatre, and Nikolay Solovtsov, who was to create the title role in *The Bear.*

ANTON CHEKHOV'S BRIEF LIFE

In 1879 Chekhov moved to Moscow to enter the medical school at the university, funded by a scholarship from the Taganrog municipal authorities. He arrived to find himself the head of the family, which was still in dire straits and living in a cramped basement flat in a disreputable slum. His father, now a humble clerk in a suburban warehouse, boarded at his office; Aleksandr, a journalist, and Nikolay, a painter, led alcoholic and bohemian lives; his three younger siblings, Ivan, Mariya, and Mikhail, still had to complete their educations. Lodging at home, Chekhov was compelled to carve out a career as a journalist at the same time that he was taking the rigorous five-year course in medicine.

At first, he wrote primarily for humor magazines, contributing anecdotes and extended jokes, sometimes as captions to drawings by Nikolay and others; these brought in a niggardly ten to twelve kopeks a line. Gradually, he diversified into parodies, short stories, and serials, including a murder mystery, *The Shooting Party*, and a romance that proved so popular it was filmed several times in the days of silent cinema (*Futile Victory*). He was a reporter at the trial of the CEOs of a failed bank. He became a close friend of Nikolay Leykin, editor of the periodical *Splinters of Petersburg Life*, to which he was a regular contributor from 1883. He conducted a theatrical gossip column, which won him entry to all the greenrooms and side-scenes in Moscow. And he partook of his brothers' bohemianism. He wrote to an old school chum in a letter his Soviet editors provided only in expurgated form: "I was on a spree all last night and, 'cept for a 3-ruble drunk didn't . . . or catch . . . I'm just about to go on a spree again."[5] His writing at this time was published under a variety of pseudonyms, the best known being Antosha Chekhonte, from a schoolboy nickname. He also found time to revise *Without Patrimony*, which he seriously hoped would be staged; turned down by the leading actress to whom he submitted it, it was burnt by its author. Chekhov always took failure in the theater hard. However, two variant copies survived, minus the title page. It was first published in 1923. It has since become known as *Platonov*, after the central character.

The year 1884 was critical in Chekhov's life. At the age of twenty-four, he set up as a general practitioner and, influenced by reading the English social critic Herbert Spencer, began research on a history of medicine in Russia. That December he had bouts of spitting blood, which his medical expertise might have led him to diagnose as a symptom of pulmonary tuberculosis. No outside observer would have suspected this active, well-built, handsome young man was suffering from a mortal illness. Only in his last years did he become a semi-invalid, and, until that time, he kept up the pretence that his symptoms were not fatal. This subterfuge was not carried on simply to allay his family's anxieties. He wilfully strove to ignore the forecast of his own mortality and regularly discounted the gravity of his condition.

Eighteen eighty-four also saw the publication of his first collection of stories, pointedly entitled *Fairy Tales of Melpomene*: the muse of tragedy compressed into pithy anecdotes of the life of actors. Chekhov had found more prestigious and better-paying periodicals to take his stories and was now an expert on Moscow life.

He had an opportunity to amplify his subject matter when he and his family began to spend summers in the country, first with his brother Ivan, master of a village school, and then in a cottage on the estate of the Kiselyov family. It was during those summers that Chekhov gained first-hand knowledge of the manor house setting he employed in many of his plays, and made the acquaintance of the officers of a battery, who turn up as characters in *Three Sisters*. Chekhov's artistic horizons also expanded, for the Kiselyovs, intimates of the composer Chaikovsky, were devoted to classical music. Another summer visitor to become a lifelong friend was the painter Isaak Levitan, whose impressionistic landscapes are graphic counterparts of Chekhov's descriptions.

The following year Chekhov's literary career took a conspicuous upward turn. On a visit to St. Petersburg, Chekhov had been embarrassed by the acclaim that greeted him, because he recognized that much of his output had been hasty and unrevised. "If I had known that that was how they were reading me," he wrote his brother Aleksandr, on January 4, 1886, "I would not have written like a hack." Such stories as "Grief" and "The Huntsman," both from 1885, had already displayed a new care in technique and seriousness in subject matter. Shortly thereafter, he received a letter from Dmitry Grigorovich, the *doyen* of Russian critics, singling him out as the most promising writer of his time and urging him to take his talent more seriously. Although Antosha Chekhonte continued to appear in print for a few more years, Anton Chekhov made his first bow in the powerful Petersburg newspaper *New Times*. Its editor, Aleksey Suvorin, had risen from peasant origins to become a tycoon and a leading influence-monger in the conservative political camp. He and Chekhov were to be closely allied, although their friendship would later founder when Suvorin promoted the anti-Semitic line during the Dreyfus affair.

During the years when he was winning recognition as a writer of short stories, Chekhov made two further attempts to write for the theater. With the first, *Along the Highway* (1885), he came up against the obstacle of the censor, who banned it on the grounds that it was a "gloomy, squalid play." The other piece, the monologue *The Evils of Tobacco*, was, like many of his early "dramatic études," written with a specific actor in mind. It first appeared in 1886 in a St. Petersburg newspaper, and Chekhov kept revising it, publishing the final version, virtually a new work, in his collected writings of 1903. Farces he sketched out with collaborators never got beyond the planning stage.

Between 1886 and 1887, Chekhov published one hundred and sixty-six titles while practicing medicine. Such fecundity boosted his fame but wore him out. His health and his temper both began to fray. Profiting from an advance from Suvorin, Chekhov returned to southern Russia in 1887, a trip that produced remarkable work. The stories that ensued signaled his emergence as a leading writer of serious fiction. The novella "The Steppe" (1888) was published in *The Northern Herald*, one of the so-called fat, or weighty, journals that had introduced the writing of Ivan Turgenev and Lev Tolstoy and served as organs of public opinion. That same year, Chekhov was awarded the Pushkin Prize for Literature by the Imperial Academy of Science for his collection *In the Gloaming*. One of the most enthusiastic instigators of this honor had been the writer Vladimir Nemirovich-Danchenko, who would later play an important role in establishing Chekhov's reputation as a dramatist.

The Northern Herald was liberal in its politics, its editor, Aleksey Pleshcheev, a former prisoner in Siberia with Dostoevsky. Typically, Chekhov was able to be friendly with Pleshcheev and Suvorin at the same time, and he continued to contribute to *New Times*. His reluctance to be identified with any one faction exposed him to much acrimonious criticism from members of both camps, and especially from the progressive left. The writer Katherine Mansfield pointed out that the "problem" in literature is an invention of the nineteenth century. One of the legacies of Russian "civic criticism" of the 1840s was the notion that a writer had an obligation to engage with social problems and offer solutions, making his works an uplifting instrument of enlightenment. This usually meant espousing a doctrinaire political platform. Chekhov, perhaps fortified by his medical training, treasured his objectivity and steadfastly refrained from taking sides, even when his sympathies were easy to ascertain. "God keep us from generalizations," he wrote. "There are a great many opinions in this world and a good half of them are professed by people who have never had any problems."

Between 1886 and 1890, his letters discuss his objectivity and his "monthly change" of opinions, which readers preferred to see as the views of his leading characters. To his brother Aleksandr he insisted on May 10, 1886, that in writing no undue emphasis be placed on political, social, or economic questions. In another letter to Suvorin, on October 27, 1888, Chekhov wrote that the author must be an observer, posing questions but not supplying the answers. It is the reader who brings subjectivity to bear. Not that an author should be aloof, but his own involvement in a problem should be invisible to the reader, he explained to Suvorin, on April 1, 1890:

> You reproach me for my objectivity, calling it indifference to good and evil, absence of ideals and ideas, etc. You want me to say, when I depict horse thieves: horse-stealing is a bad thing. But that's been known for a long time now, without my help, hasn't it? Let juries pass verdicts on horse thieves; as for me, my work is only to show them as they are.

The year before "The Steppe" appeared, Chekhov had at last had a play produced; the manager Fyodor Korsh had commissioned *Ivanov* and staged it at his Moscow theater on November 19, 1887. It was a decided if controversial success. As Chekhov wrote to Aleksandr, "Theater buffs say they've never seen so much ferment, so much unanimous applause *cum* hissing, and never ever heard so many arguments as they saw and heard at my play" (November 20, 1887). It was taken up by the Alexandra Theatre, the Imperial dramatic playhouse in St. Petersburg, and produced there on January 31, 1889, after much hectic rewriting in an attempt to make the playwright's intentions clearer and to take into account the strengths and weaknesses of the new cast.

The theme of a protagonist fettered by a sick wife and want of money was a distorted reflection of Chekhov's own situation. His family obligations kept his nose to the grindstone, and he felt guilty whenever he traveled away. Yet the success of *Ivanov* and the curtain-raisers *The Bear* and *The Proposal* (1888–1889) had put Chekhov at a premium as a dramatist. Urged on by Korsh and others, and unable to make headway on a full-length novel, Chekhov hoped to collaborate with Suvorin on a new comedy; when the publisher begged off, Chekhov completed it himself as *The Wood Goblin* (1889). It was promptly turned down by the state-subsidized theaters of Petersburg and Moscow, which regarded it as more a dramatized story than an actable play. They recommended that Chekhov give up writing for the stage. A production at a private theater in Moscow was received with apathy bordering on contempt, and may have helped provide the impetus for a decision Chekhov would soon make to go to Sakhalin, ten thousand miles away. Throughout 1888 and 1889, Chekhov also tended to his brother Nikolay, who was dying of tuberculosis; after Nikolay's death, Chekhov experienced both guilt and a foreboding of his own mortality, which brought on the mood conveyed in "A Dismal Story" (1889), in which a professor of medicine contemplates his frustrated ideals and imminent demise. The author's mood was at its lowest ebb.

Secure in his reputation and income at the age of thirty, Chekhov sought to cast off this despondency by traveling to Sakhalin, the Russian Devil's Island, in 1890; the eighty-one-day journey was arduous, for the Trans-Siberian railway had not yet been built. The enterprise may have been inspired by a Tolstoyan wish to practice altruism or it may have been an ambitious project to write a magnum opus of "medical geography." In any case, the ensuing documentary study of the penal colony was a model of socially engaged field research, and may have led to prison reforms. On a more personal level, it intensified a new strain of pessimism in Chekhov's work, for, despite his disclaimers, he began to be bothered by his lack of outlook or mission.

No sooner had Chekhov returned, via Hong Kong, Singapore, and Ceylon, than he made his first excursion to Western Europe, accompanying Suvorin. His initial enthusiasm for Vienna, Venice, and Naples began to wane by the time he visited Nice, Monte Carlo, and Paris, and he was eager to get back to work. In Russia, with the writing routines resumed, the sense of enslavement returned. This mood was modulated by a flirtation with a family friend, Lidiya (Lika) Mizinova, who invested more significance in the relationship than he did. Her subsequent affair and illegitimate child with the married writer Ignaty Potapenko would be exploited by Chekhov in *The Seagull* (although he hoped his own circle would not spot the similarities).

The steady flow of royalties enabled Chekhov in 1891 to buy a farmstead at Melikhovo, some fifty miles south of Moscow, where he settled his parents and siblings. There he set about "to squeeze the last drop of slave out of his system" (as he wrote to Suvorin on January 7, 1889); "a modern Cincinnatus," he planted a cherry orchard, installed a flush toilet, and became a lavish host. This rustication had a beneficial effect on both his literary work and his humanitarianism. He threw himself into schemes for building roads and schools and opened a clinic to provide free medical treatment, improving peasants' minds and bodies. During the cholera epidemic of 1892–1893, he served as an overworked member of the sanitary commission and head of the famine relief board. These experiences found their way into the activities of Dr. Astrov in *Uncle Vanya*.

During this period, Chekhov composed masterful stories that explored the dead ends of life: "The Duel" (1891), "Ward No. 6" (1892), "The Black Monk," "A Woman's Kingdom," "The Student" (all 1894), "Three Years" (1895), "The House with the Mansard," "My Life" (both 1896), and "Peasants" (1897), carefully wrought prose pieces of great psychological subtlety. They recurrently dwell on the illusions indispensable to making life bearable, the often frustrated attempts at contact with one's fellow man, the inexorable pull of inertia preventing people from realizing their potential for honesty and happiness. Chekhov's attitude is clinically critical, but always with a keen eye for the sympathetic details that lead the reader to a deeper understanding.

For several years, Chekhov abandoned the theater, except for some monologues and one-act farces. Not until January 1894 did he announce that he had again begun a play, only to deny it a year later, in a letter to V. V. Bilibin: "I am not writing a play and, altogether, I have no inclination to write any. I am grown old, and I have lost my burning ardor. I should like to write a novel 100 miles long" (January 18, 1895). Nine months after that he was to break the news to Suvorin, "Can you imagine, I am writing a play which I shall probably not finish before the end of November. I am writing it not without pleasure, though I swear horribly at the conventions of the stage. A comedy, three women's parts, six men's, four acts, a landscape (view of a lake); a great deal of conversation about literature, little action, five tons of love" (October 21, 1895).

The comedy was *The Seagull*, which had a rocky opening night at St. Petersburg's Alexandra Theatre in 1896: the actors misunderstood it, the audience misapprehended it. Despite protestations of unconcern to Suvorin ("I dosed myself with castor oil, took a cold bath—and now I would not even mind writing another play"; October 22, 1896), Chekhov fled to Melikhovo, where he renounced playwriting. Although *The Seagull* grew in public favor in subsequent performances, Chekhov disliked submitting his work to the judgment of literary cliques and claques. Yet barely one year after the event, a new drama from his hand appeared in the 1897 collection of his plays: *Uncle Vanya*, a reworking of the earlier *The Wood Goblin*. It was widely performed in provincial capitals, where the residents found it reflected their dreary lives.

It was during this year that Chekhov's illness was definitively diagnosed as tuberculosis, and he was compelled to leave Melikhovo for a milder climate. For the rest of his life, he shuttled between Yalta on the Black Sea and various French and German spas, with occasional business trips to Moscow. He had a house constructed in the Yalta suburb of Autka. To pay for it, and to cover the new expenses his multiple residences created, Chekhov sold all he had written before 1899, excepting the plays, to the publisher Marks for the flat fee of 75,000 rubles (in current purchasing power, approximately $81,000), along with the reprint rights to any future stories. It was an improvident move. Marks had had no idea of the size of Chekhov's output and had underpaid. The error in calculation may have induced Chekhov to return to playwriting as a more lucrative activity.

The remainder of his dramatic career was bound up with the fortunes of the Moscow Art Theatre, founded in 1897 by his friend Nemirovich-Danchenko and the wealthy dilettante K. S. Alekseev, who acted under the name Konstantin Stanislavsky. Chekhov was one of the original shareholders in the enterprise. He admired his friends' announced program of ensemble playing, their serious attitude to art, and a repertory of high literary quality. At the opening production, Aleksey Tolstoy's blank-verse historical drama *Tsar Feodor Ioannovich*, his eye was caught by Olga Knipper, the young actress who played the tsarina. With only slight misgivings Chekhov allowed the Art Theatre to revive *The Seagull* at the close of its first season. Stanislavsky, as co-director, had greater misgivings; he did not understand the play. But a heavily atmospheric production won over the audience, and the play was a resounding success. The Moscow Art Theatre adopted an art-nouveau seagull as its insignia and henceforth regarded Chekhov as its house dramatist. When the Imperial Maly Theatre insisted on revisions to *Uncle Vanya*, which had been playing throughout the provinces for years, Chekhov withdrew the play from them and allowed the Art Theatre to stage its Moscow premiere. *Three Sisters* (1901) was written with Art Theatre actors in mind.

Chekhov's chronic reaction to the production of his plays was revulsion, and so two months after the opening of *Three Sisters*, he was declaring, to Olga Knipper, "I will never write for the theater again. One can write for the theater in Germany, in Sweden, even in Spain, but not in Russia, where dramatists get no respect, are kicked by hooves and forgiven neither success nor failure"

(March 1, 1901). Nevertheless, he soon was deep into *The Cherry Orchard* (1904), tailoring the roles to specific Moscow Art players. Each of these productions won Chekhov greater fame as a playwright, even when he himself disagreed with the chosen interpretation of the Art Theatre.

Chekhov languished in Yalta, which he called his "warm Siberia," feeling that he had been shunted to an outpost for the moribund. At the age of forty, in 1900, to the great surprise of his friends and the temporary dismay of his sister Mariya, who had always been his housekeeper, he married the Art Theatre actress Olga Knipper. Chekhov's liaisons with women had been numerous, ranging from a brief engagement in 1886 to Dunya Efros, a Jewish woman who refused to convert to Orthodoxy, to a one-night stand with a Japanese prostitute and a fling with the flamboyant actress Lidiya Yavorskaya. He exercised an involuntary fascination over a certain type of ambitious bluestocking and his fan mail from female admirers was considerable. Some women friends, such as Lidiya Avilova, projected their desires onto an ordinary relationship, casting themselves as Chekhov's Egeria. Whenever the affair became too demanding or the woman too clinging, Chekhov would use irony and playful humor to disengage himself. In his writings, marriage is usually portrayed as a snare and a delusion that mires his characters in spirit-sapping vulgarity. His relationship with Knipper was both high-spirited—she was his "kitten," his "horsie," his "lambkin," his "darling crocodile"—and conveniently remote, for she had to spend much of her time in Moscow, while he convalesced at his villa in Yalta. On those terms, the marriage was a success.

Chekhov's villa, today a museum, became a Mecca for young writers, importunate fans, touring acting companies, and plain freeloaders. Such pilgrimages, though well meant, were not conducive to Chekhov's peace of mind or body, and his health continued to deteriorate. Despite this rapid decline, and the disappointment of a miscarriage Olga suffered in 1902,[6] a deeply lyrical tone suffuses his last writings. His late stories, "The Darling" and "Lady with Lapdog" (both 1899) and "The Bishop" (1902) and "Betrothed" (1903), offer more acceptance of the cyclical nature of life. They also reveal an almost musical attention to the structure and sounds of words, a quality to be remarked as well in the last "comedy," *The Cherry Orchard*.

In December 1903, a failing Chekhov came to Moscow to attend rehearsals of *The Cherry Orchard*. The opening night, January 17, 1904, concided with his name day and the twenty-fifth anniversary of the commencement of his literary activity. Emaciated, hunched over, gravely ill, he did not show up until the second act and sat through the third, after which, to his great bemusement, a ceremony to honor him took place.

In June 1904 the Berlin doctors Chekhov consulted ordered him to Badenweiler, a health resort in the Black Forest. There the forty-four-year-old writer died on July 2. Shortly before his death, the doctor recommended putting an ice pack on his heart. "You don't put ice on an empty heart," Chekhov protested. When they suggested a glass of champagne, his last words came, "It's been a long time since I've drunk champagne." Unconsciously, he echoed the line of the old nurse Marina in *Uncle Vanya*: "It's a long time since I've had noodles."

Chekhov's obsequies were a comedy of errors he might have appreciated. The railway carriage bearing his body to St. Petersburg was stencilled with the label "Fresh Oysters," and, at the Novodevichy cemetery in Moscow, the bystanders spent more time ogling the controversial author Maksim Gorky and the bass singer Fyodor Shalyapin than in mourning the deceased.[7] Finally, and inadvertently, Chekhov's cortège became entangled with that of General Keller, a military hero who had been shipped home from the Far East. Chekhov's friends were startled to hear an army band accompanying the remains of a man who had always been chary of the grand gesture.

NOTES

1 The date given by Chekhov himself, although he would appear to have been born on the 16th. The 17th was his "saint's day" or "name day," the day of St. Anthony after whom he was christened. Dates given here are "Old Style," in accord with the Julian calendar, twelve days behind the Gregorian.

2 M. P. Chekhov, *Vokrug Chekhova* (Moscow: Moskovsky rabochy, 1980), p. 44.

3 Quoted in Ernest Simmons, *Chekhov, A Biography* (Boston: Little, Brown, 1962), p. 6.

4 Peter the Great had established a table of ranks that stratified social status into civil, military, naval, and ecclesiastical hierarchies. In the civil hierarchy, *meshchanin* (literally, townsman) came just above peasant. In *The Seagull*, Treplyov complains that his father had been classified as a *meshchanin* of Kiev, even though he was a famous actor, and the same rank appears on his own passport. He finds it particularly galling since the term had come to imply philistinism.

5 Letter to Dmitry Savelyov, January (?) 1884. All translated quotations from Chekhov's writings and letters are based on *Polnoe sobranie sochineny i pisem*, the complete collected works and letters in thirty volumes published in Moscow in

1974–1983. On the cuts made by Soviet editors, see A. Chudakov, " 'Neprilich-nye slova' i oblik klassika. O kupyurakh v izdaniya pisem Chekhova," *Literaturnoe obozrenie* (November 1991): 54–56.

6 Olga's miscarriage is described in a letter of hers to Chekhov (March 31, 1902). However, a controversy has arisen among scholars as to whether it was a mis-carriage, an ectopic pregnancy, or something else; moreover, the paternity of the child has been questioned. See the articles of Hugh McLean and Donald Rayfield in *The Bulletin of the North American Chekhov Society* XI, 1 (Summer 2003), and letters in subsequent issues.

7 Maksim Gorky, *Literary Portraits*, trans. Ivy Litvinov (Moscow: Foreign Lan-guages Publishing House, n.d.), pp. 158–159.

CHRONOLOGY OF CHEKHOV'S LIFE

1860. *January 17* (Old Style) / *29* (New Style). Anton Pavlovich Chekhov, third son of the shopkeeper and choirmaster Pavel Yegorovich Chekhov and Yevgeniya Yakovlevna Morozova, is born in Taganrog, a port of the Sea of Azov. He is the grandson of a serf who managed to purchase his liberation.

Aleksandr Ostrovsky's play *Thunderstorm* wins an award from the Academy of Sciences

1861. Tsar Alexander II abolishes serfdom, but without providing enough land for the emancipated serfs.

1862. Ivan Turgenev's *Fathers and Sons* is published.

Academic freedom restored to Russian universities.

1863. Flogging with birch rods abolished by law.

Konstantin Stanislavsky is born, as Konstantin Alekseev, son of a wealthy textile manufacturer.

Nikolay Chernyshevsky's *What Is to Be Done?*, the gospel of nihilism, is written in prison.

1864. *Zemstvos*, self-governing rural councils, are created.

1865. Lev Tolstoy begins to publish *War and Peace*.

[33]

1866. An attempted assassination of the tsar prompts a wave of political reaction, especially in education and the press. Chekhov, as a student, will suffer from the new emphasis on Greek, Latin, and grammar.

Fyodor Dostoevsky's *Crime and Punishment* published.

1867–1879. Chekhov's primary and secondary education in Taganrog in very rigorous schools. He gives lessons, frequents the theater, edits a student newspaper, writes plays now lost.

1868. Dostoevsky's *The Idiot* is published serially.

1871. Dostoevsky's *The Devils* is published.

1872. Special court set up to try treason cases.

1873. Only 227 factories in all of Russia.

Nikolay Nekrasov begins to publish his populist poem *Who Can Be Happy in Russia?*

1874. Trade unions made illegal.

All males over twenty-one, regardless of class, now liable for conscription into the armed forces.

1875. Chekhov writes comic journal *The Stutterer* to amuse his brothers in Moscow.

Tolstoy begins to publish *Anna Karenina.*

1876. Chekhov's father goes bankrupt and moves the family to Moscow, leaving Anton in Taganrog.

1877. Chekhov visits Moscow where he finds his family in penury.

The Russians fight the Turks in the Balkans, ostensibly to free the Christian Slavs from Moslem oppression. An armistice, signed in 1878, greatly reduces the Turkish presence in the Balkans, but the Congress of Berlin humiliates Russia by reducing its spoils to part of Bessarabia.

1878. Chekhov writes plays now lost: *Without Patrimony, He Met His Match*, and *The Hen Has Good Reason to Cluck*.

Public outcries against the government and acts of terrorism increase.

1879. Chekhov finishes high school and in June moves to Moscow, where he enrolls in the medical school of the University of Moscow on a scholarship. Starts to write cartoon captions for the humor magazine *Alarm Clock*.

Dostoevsky begins to publish *The Brothers Karamazov*.

1880. *March.* Chekhov's first short story, "Letter of a Landowner to His Learned Neighbor Dr. Friedrich," is published in the comic journal *The Dragon-fly*.

1880–1887. Chekhov writes for Moscow and St. Petersburg comic journals under pen names including Antosha Chekhonte, Doctor Who's Lost His Patients, Man without a Spleen, and My Brother's Brother.

1881. Chekhov writes play later known as *Platonov* (not published until 1923).

Tsar Alexander II is assassinated; his son, Alexander III, initiates a reign of political repression and social stagnation.

Dostoevsky dies.

1882. *Platonov* is turned down by the Maly Theatre. Chekhov publishes "Late-blooming Flowers."

The imperial monopoly on theater in Moscow and St. Petersburg is abolished. Several private theaters are opened.

Troops are used to suppress student uprisings at the Universities of St. Petersburg and Kazan.

1883. Chekhov publishes "Fat and Lean," "At Sea," and "Christmas Eve."

1884. Chekhov finishes his medical studies and starts general practice in Chikino, outside Moscow. Publishes his first collection of stories, *Fairy Tales of Melpomene*, under the name Antosha Chekhonte. His only attempt at a novel, *The Shooting Party*, serialized in *Daily News*. Writes one-act play, *Along the High Road*, which is censored and not published until 1914.

December. Symptoms of Chekhov's tuberculosis diagnosed.

1885. Chekhov's first trip to St. Petersburg. Meets the publisher Aleksey Suvorin and the painter Isaak Levitan, who become close friends. Romances with Dunya Efros and Nataliya Golden. Publishes "The Huntsman," "Sergeant Prishibeev," and "Grief."

1886. Chekhov begins writing for Suvorin's conservative newspaper *New Times*. Puts out a second collection of stories, *Motley Tales*, signed both An. P. Chekhov and Antosha Chekhonte.

The eminent Russian critic Dmitry Grigorovich encourages him to pursue his literary career in a more serious fashion. Publishes "The Witch," "The Chorus Girl," "On the Road," and the first version of the comic monologue *The Evils of Tobacco*.

1887. Chekhov publishes third collection of short stories, *In the Gloaming*, and fourth collection, *Innocent Conversations*, which include "Enemies," "Typhus," "The Siren," and "Kashtanka." Also writes one-act *Swan Song*.

November 19. Ivanov, a full-length play, performed at Korsh's Theatre, Moscow. It receives a mixed press.

1888. First serious long story, "The Steppe," published in St. Petersburg magazine *Northern Herald*, initiating a new care taken with his writing. One-act farces *The Bear* and *The Proposal* produced to acclaim. *In the Gloaming* wins the Pushkin Prize of the Academy of Sciences.

Student uprisings at the Universities of Moscow, Odessa, Kharkov, and Kazan are put down by the military. The government decrees that all Jews must live within the Pale of Settlement in Eastern Poland and the western provinces of Russia.

Tolstoy publishes his play of peasant life *The Power of Darkness*, but the censor will not allow it to be staged.

Maksim Gorky is arrested for subversion, and is henceforth under police surveillance.

1889. The Social Democratic Working-man's Party is founded.

"A Dismal Story," one of the first of Chekhov's mature stories, published in *Northern Herald*.

January 31. Premiere of the revised *Ivanov* at Alexandra Theatre, St. Petersburg.

October. Chekhov's play *The Wood Goblin* finished. Played at Abramova's Theatre in *December*. The play is poorly received by the critics; he is scolded for "blindly copying everyday life and paying no attention to the requirements of the stage."

1890. According to a letter to Sergey Dyagilev, Chekhov reworks *The Wood Goblin* into *Uncle Vanya*, which will not be published until 1897. Chekhov publishes collection *Glum People*, which includes "Thieves" and "Gusev." Writes one-act comedies, *The Involuntary Tragedian* and *The Wedding*.

April–October. Travels through Siberia to Sakhalin Island, where he visits prison camps and carries out a census. Sails in the Pacific and Indian Oceans.

1891. Six-week trip to Western Europe. Publication of the novella *The Duel* and "Peasant Women." Buys a small farmstead in Melikhovo.

1892. Chekhov settles in Melikhovo with his family.

Work begins on the Trans-Siberian Railway, to be completed in 1905.

Sergey Witte becomes Minister of Finance, and turns Russia into a modern industrial state, increasing industrialism, railways, and Western trade by 1899.

1892–1893. Severe famines in the grain-growing provinces in the south and along the Volga.

Chekhov acts as head of the district sanitary commission during the cholera epidemic, combats the famine, treats the poorest peasants for free.

Publishes eleven stories, including "My Wife," "The Grasshopper," "Ward No. 6," as well as the one-act farce *The Celebration.*

1893. Dalliance with Lika Mizinova, whom he decides not to marry, but who sees herself as a prototype for Nina in *The Seagull.* *The Island of Sakhalin* published serially. Publishes "An Anonymous Story" and "Big Volodya and Little Volodya."

1894. Second trip to Italy and to Paris. Health worsens. Publishes "The Student," "Rothschild's Fiddle," "The Head Gardener's Story," "The Literature Teacher," "The Black Monk," and "At a Country House."

Alexander III dies and is succeeded by his son, the conservative and vacillating Nicholas II.

1895. *The Island of Sakhalin* published. Chekhov meets Lev Tolstoy at his estate Yasnaya Polyana.

Chekhov writes *The Seagull*, publishes "Three Years," "Ariadne," "His Wife," "Whitebrow," "Murder," and "Anna Round the Neck."

1896. Chekhov sponsors the construction of a primary school in the village of Talezh. Serial publication of "My Life" and "The House with a Mansard."

October 17. The premiere of *The Seagull* at the Alexandra Theatre in St. Petersburg fails. Chekhov flees during the second act.

October 21. Relative success of the play at its second performance.

1896–1897. Strikes of factory workers lead to a law limiting adult work to eleven and a half hours a day.

1897. The first All-Russian Congress of Stage Workers meets in Moscow to argue questions of trade conditions and artistic principles.

Stanislavsky and Nemirovich-Danchenko found the Moscow Art Theatre.

Chekhov sponsors the construction of a primary school in the village of Novosyolky. Participates in the All-Russian census of the population. Father dies.

March–April. Hospitalized with first acute attack of pulmonary tuberculosis. Reads Maurice Maeterlinck.

September. Travels to France for medical treatment.

Uncle Vanya, Ivanov, The Seagull, and one-act plays published, as well as stories "Peasants," "The Savage," "At Home," and "In the Cart."

1898. Thirteen thousand students at Moscow University go on strike to protest repressive moves on the part of the administration; orders are given to enlist them in the army.

May. Chekhov returns from abroad. Relations with Suvorin strained in connection with the Dreyfus trial.

September. Settles in Yalta after suffering a pulmonary hemorrhage. Publishes the stories "Calling on Friends," "Gooseberries," "About Love," "A Case History," and "Ionych."

December 17. The Seagull, staged by Stanislavsky, is revived with great success at the Moscow Art Theatre.

1899. Theatres in Kiev, Kharkov, and Nizhny Novgorod play *Uncle Vanya.* Chekhov decides to turn it into a short novel, but does not. Offered to the Maly, *Uncle Vanya* is considered offensive to professors and is turned down.

Tolstoy's *Resurrection* and Gorky's *Foma Gordeev* published.

Chekhov attends a performance of *The Seagull* in Yalta. Sells all rights to his works to the publisher A. F. Marks for 75,000 rubles (in current purchasing power, approximately $81,000). Begins to edit his complete works. Awarded Order of St. Stanislas, second class, for work in education. Publishes "On Official Business," "Lady with Lapdog," "The Darling," and "The New Villa."

June. Sells his estate in Melikhovo. Has a house built in Yalta.

October 26. Premiere of *Uncle Vanya* at the Art Theatre.

1900. *January.* Elected to honorary membership in the Literary division of the Academy of Sciences. Publishes "In the Ravine" and "At Christmas."

April. The Art Theatre plays *Uncle Vanya* and *The Seagull* in Sevastopol, in the presence of the author.

August–December. Writes *Three Sisters.* Finishes the play in Nice.

1901. *January–February.* Trip to Italy.

January 31. Premiere of *Three Sisters* at the Moscow Art Theatre with considerable success.

May 25. Marries the actress Olga Knipper, who plays Masha.

The Marxist journal *Life*, which publishes Gorky, is banned. Gorky is expelled from Nizhny Novgorod.

1902. Chekhov publishes "The Bishop." Complete works published in eleven volumes. Awarded Griboedov Prize of Society of Dramatic Authors and Opera Composers for *Three Sisters*. Begins *The Cherry Orchard.*

March. Olga Knipper suffers miscarriage.

August. Resigns in protest from the Academy of Sciences when Gorky's election is nullified at the tsar's behest.

Gorky writes *The Lower Depths.*

1903. At a Congress in London, the Social Democratic Working-man's Party is taken over by the radical Bolshevist wing, led by Vladimir Lenin.

Second edition of Chekhov's complete works published in sixteen volumes.

Publishes his last story, "Betrothed," in the magazine *Everybody's.*

June. The censor rules that his plays cannot be performed in people's theaters, low-priced theater for the working class.

September. The Cherry Orchard is finished. Nemirovich-Danchenko and Stanislavsky are enthusiastic. Chekhov attends rehearsals.

An atrocious pogrom occurs in Kishinyov, with 47 dead and 2,000 families ruined.

1904. Chekhov's health deteriorates.

January 14 or 15. Attends a rehearsal of *The Cherry Orchard.*

January 17. Premiere at the Art Theatre, where a celebration in his honor is held.

Spring. A new, grave attack of tuberculosis.

April 2. First performance of *Orchard* in St. Petersburg a great success, greater than in Moscow, according to Nemirovich and Stanislavsky.

June 1. Publication of the play in a separate edition by Marks.

June 3. Departure for Germany with Olga Knipper.

July 2/15. Dies in Badenweiler.

July 9/22. Buried in Novo-devichy cemetery in Moscow.

The Mensheviks drive the Bolsheviks from the Central Committee of the Social Democratic Working-man's Party, but drop out the following year, leaving the field to the Bolsheviks.

The Russo-Japanese war breaks out.

1909. First performance of a Chekhov play in English: *The Seagull,* translated by George Calderon, at the Glasgow Repertory Theatre.

A NOTE ON THE TRANSLATION

The text on which this translation is based is that in A. P. Chekhov, *Polnoe sobranie sochineniy i pisem v tridtsati tomakh* (*Complete Works and Letters in Thirty Volumes*), edited by N. F. Belchikov et al. (Moscow: Nauka, 1974–1984). The Russian text was drawn from the latest version published in Chekhov's lifetime and subject to his revision.

Chekhov had his doubts about the efficacy of translation, and after reading some Russian prose translated into French, concluded that transmission of Russian literature into another language was pointless. Later, when his own plays began to be translated, he lamented that purely Russian phenomena would have no meaning for foreign audiences. To offset these misgivings, the translator of Chekhov must be as sedulous in making choices as the author was in composing the original work.

From his earliest farces, Chekhov wrote plays with an eye to their being performed. He often had specific actors in mind, and, despite his discomfort with histrionic convention, he expected his dialogue to be recited from the stage. Therefore, translating his plays entails problems different from those encountered in translating his prose fiction. At first sight, the vocabulary and sentence structure seem straightforward enough. Under scrutiny, however, the seeming simplicity turns out to be illusory.

The literary psychoanalyst Gregory Zilboorg, initiating American readers into Russian drama in 1920, stated point-blank that Chekhov was fundamentally untranslatable, more so even than Aleksandr Ostrovsky and Maksim Gorky. "Chekhov's plays lose their chief element in translation into whatever other language: the particular harmony and rhythm of the original. The student must bear in mind that studying Chekhov's drama in English he actually studies only some elements of them, the rest being lost in a foreign language."[1]

The "harmony and rhythm" so lost derive from a number of sources. First, Chekhov uses language to consolidate his major plays: recurrent phrases echo off one another, often for ironic effect. George Bernard Shaw was another playwright well aware that it was precisely this adhesive repetition of key words that knit a play together. He scolded his German translator,

> The way in which you translate every word just as it comes and then forget it and translate it some other way when it begins (or should begin) to make the audience laugh, is enough to whiten the hair on an author's head. Have you ever read Shakespear's Much Ado About Nothing? In it a man calls a constable an ass, and throughout the rest of the play the constable can think of nothing but this insult and keeps on saying, "But forget not, mas-

ters, that I am an ass." Now if you translated Much Ado, you would make the man call the constable a Schaffkopf. On the next page he would be a Narr, then a Maul, then a Thier, and perhaps the very last time an Esel.[2]

This was such a salient principle for Shaw that he hammered at it the following month: "I tell you again and again most earnestly and seriously, that unless you repeat the words that I have repeated, you will throw away all the best stage effects and make the play unpopular with the actors . . . Half the art of dialogue consists in the echoing of words—the tossing back & forwards of phrases from one to another like a cricket ball . . ."[3]

What is true for Shaw is equally true for Chekhov. In Chekhov, a commonplace uttered in the first act may return to resonate with fresh significance. In *The Cherry Orchard*, changes are constantly being rung on *neschastye* (unhappiness, misfortune, trouble). Other words are not so much thematic as atmospheric: Yasha twice calls Dunyasha "a tasty little pickle" (*ogurchik*) and the vegetable is repeated in Pishchik's bucket of pickles and even (as a gesture) Charlotta Ivanovna's gnawing on a pickle. In Act One, Varya describes a religious pilgrimage as "Heavenly!"; in Act Three, Trofimov uses the same word to mock her. It is the translator's obligation to preserve these *leitmotifs* as much as possible.

Lexical and etymological elements subliminally affect the atmosphere. Earthy terms, such as *nedotyopa* (half-chopped) and *vrazdrob* (chopped to bits) contribute to the theme of hewing down the cherry trees. Literary allusions enrich the cultural context, although in this play they usually function as a joke. Gaev's reference to the Decadents, Epikhodov's appeal to Buckle, Pish-chik's remark about Nietzsche all indicate the distance of the characters from the intellectual world of their referents. The vagrant's quotations from the poems of Nadson and Nekrasov make a fraudulent appeal to progressive reform, so should sound empty in their rhetoric.

In his last plays, Chekhov is extremely careful in choosing his words. Every character in Chekhov speaks in a particu-lar cadence. Compare Pishchik's short asthmatic phrases with Gaev's run-on grandiloquence or Anya's iambic meters with Trofimov's spondaics. Firs's curt speech features blunt peasant terms, Charlotta Ivanovna's foreignness is apparent in her sen-tence structure, and Epikhodov's autodidacticism is proclaimed by the "ten-dollar words" misapprehended from his reading.

Harder to pin down is that the "specific gravity" of a statement may reside in its structure. Russian can reassemble the elements of a sentence to make a particular emphasis; English has to find a way of reproducing this. Mere phrasebook translation, offering a direct statement, can betray the subtle emphases of the origi-nal. To render Charlotta Ivanovna's "*Uzhasno poyut éti lyudi*" as "These people sing horribly" is to miss her idiosyncratic syntax and the course of her thought as a foreigner which implies "It's awful the way these people break into song at the drop of a hat" (although to spell that out explicitly would be to over-translate).

Finally, certain words and phrases that once held a special meaning in Chekhov's time may require that an explanation be embedded in the translation, particularly if it is meant to be performed. Although a dictionary will tell you that *gorokhi* means peas, what Varya is feeding the old folks is not the delicacy of green peas (known in Russian as "sweet peas"), but the unpalatable dried form; hence, "beans" is a preferable choice of translation. (Similarly, Pishchik and Charlotta do not eat raw cucumbers, but pickled gherkins.)

These peculiarities of Chekhov add to the usual problems experienced in translating from Russian: the passive constructions, the distinction between verbs of imperfect and perfect action, and onomatopoeic sounds that are overlooked or scanted. Russian, an inflected language, has an ability to reorganize words in order to convey emphasis or effect. Act One ends with Trofimov's rhapsodic *"Solntse moya! Vesna moya!,"* literally, "My sun! My spring!," but to replicate the poetic effect one must draw out the line and try to re-create the sonic repetition: "My sunshine! My springtime!"

"The shock of the new" in Chekhov's handling of dialogue contributed mightily to his reputation in his lifetime, but today this aspect tends to be lost or overlooked. As Nils Åke Nilsson pointed out, Chekhov is an unacknowledged precursor of the Futurists and their launching of a *zaumny,* or transrational language. He cites as examples the phrase "You've Gavril-ed it up enough" in *Ivanov,* the trom-tom-tom exchange in *Three Sisters,* and Gaev's billiard jargon, calling this a "new dramatic syntax."[4]

The American critic Stark Young, when he set out to translate *The Seagull* for the Lunts in 1938, singled out "those balances, repetitions for stage effect, repetitions for stage economy, theatrical combinations and devices, time-patterns, and so on, that are the fruits of much intention and technical craft, and that are almost totally absent from the translation."[5] Yet even he trembled before Chekhov's linguistic audacity: "Chekhov's dialogue is perhaps a trifle more colloquial than mine. Certainly it is more colloquial than I should ever dare to be; for in a translation any very marked colloquialism is always apt to hurt the economy of effect by raising questions as to what the original could have been to come out so patly as that."

Consequently, Young was very cautious in rendering the jokiness of Chekhov's dialogue and sought a simplicity that denatures the special flavor of the language. In this respect, Chekhov is very deceptive. His lexical choices and often straightforward syntax enable him to be used in the classroom, but this seeming simplicity overlies a deliberate restriction of vocabulary. Consequently, unusual words and phrases stand out all the more. In addition, the sentence structure is organized poetically in order to express character and, as an actor of the time would put it, make points. Translators, led astray by Chekhov's poker-faced approach (in some respects similar to Mark Twain's), have often made him sound more wooden and monotonous, less fruity and lyrical, than he is.

Finally, I have not tried to pretend that Chekhov is anything other than Russian. Although I have converted weights and measures into Western equivalents so that an audience can more easily gauge distances and density, I have left currency, beverages, and, in particular, names in their Russian forms. Modern readers and audiences rapidly adjust to patronymics, diminutives, and nicknames. If one is to turn Lyubov into Lovey or Aimée and Yasha into Jake, then one must go the whole hog and refer to Firs as Thyrsus and, to be consistent, *Uncle Vanya* as *Uncle Jack*.

NOTES

1 Gregory Zilboorg, "A course in Russian drama," *The Drama* (Nov. 1920): 69.

2 *Bernard Shaw's Letters to Siegfried Trebitsch*, ed. Samuel A. Weiss (Stanford: Stanford University Press, 1986), p. 30 (26 Dec. 1902). The words translate as "sheep's head," "fool," "muzzle," "beast," "ass."

3 Ibid., 15 Jan. 1903, p. 36.

4 Nils Åke Nilsson, "Two Chekhovs: Mayakovskiy on Chekhov's 'futurism,'" in Jean-Pierre Barricelli, ed., *Chekhov's Great Plays: A Critical Anthology* (New York: New York University Press, 1981), pp. 251–61.

5 Stark Young, "Translating *The Sea Gull*," in *The Sea Gull, A Drama in Four Acts*, translated from the Russian of Anton Chekhov by Stark Young (New York: Samuel French, 1950), pp. xii–xv.

6 Ibid., p. xix.

PRONUNCIATION GUIDE

Lyubov Andreevna Ranevskaya *lyoo-BAWF ahn-DRAY-ehf-nah rahn-YEHF-sky-ah*

Lyuba *LYOO-bah*

Anya *AHN-yah*

Anichka *AHN-eech-kah*

Varya *VAHR-yah*

Varvara Mikhailovna *vahr-VAHR-ah mee-'HEIL-ahf-nah*

Leonid Andreich Gaev *lyaw-NEED ahn-DRAY-eech GUY-ehf*

Lyonya *LYAWN-yah*

Yermolay Alekseich Lopakhin *yehr-mah-LIE as-lik-SAY-eetch lah-PAH-'heen*

Pyotr Trofimov *PYAW-tr trah-FEE-mahf*

Petya *PIT-yah*

Semeonov-Pishchik *seem-YAWN-ahf PEESH-cheek*

Charlotta Ivanova *shahr-LAW-tah ee-VAHN-ahf-nah*

Semyon Panteleich Yepikhodov *sim-YAWN pahn-til-YAY-eech ippy-'HAW-dahf*

Avdotya Fydorovna *ahv-DAWT-yah FYAW-dahr-ahf-nah*

Dunyasha *doon-YA-sha*

Firs Nikolaevich *FEERSS nee-kaw-LYE-yeh-veech*

Yasha *YAH-shah*

Dashenka *DAH-shin-kah*

Fyodor Kozoedov *FYAW-dahr kah-zah-YAY-dahf*

Mentone *mawn-TONE*

Kharkov *'HARH-kawf*

Petrusha *pit-ROO-shah*

Anastasy *ah-nah-STAHSS-ee*

Grisha *GREE-shah*

Yaroslavl *yah-rah-SLAHV-l*

Yefimushka *YEH-feem-oosh-kah*

Karp *KAHRP*

Polya *PAWL-yah*

Yevstigney *iv-steeg-NAY*

Deriganov *dir-ee-GAHN-ahf*

Yegor *ye-GAWR*

Znoikov *ZNOY-kahf*

Kardamonov *kahr-dah-MAWN-ahf*

Yashnevo *YAHSH-ni-vah*

Ragulins *rah-GOO-leenz*

Volga *VAWL-gah*

INTRODUCTION

"The next play I write will definitely be funny, very funny, at least in concept," Chekhov declared to his wife on March 7, 1901, after his previous play, *Three Sisters*, had opened at the Moscow Art Theatre, following a rehearsal period in which Chekhov had argued that the play was not the tragedy the actors assumed it was. The concept for the new play, as the author sketched it to Stanislavsky, would incorporate a footman mad about fishing, a garrulous one-armed billiard player, and a situation in which a landowner is continually borrowing money from the footman. He also envisaged a branch of flowering cherry thrust through a window of the manor house.

Chekhov's notebooks reveal that *The Cherry Orchard* had taken root even earlier, with the governess Charlotta, another farcical type, and the idea that "the estate will soon go under the hammer" the next ramification. The theme had a personal application. For the boy Chekhov, the sale of his home after his father's bankruptcy had been painful. The imminent loss of one's residence looms over his early plays, becomes the impulse of

Uncle Vanya, in which an estate may be sold out from under its inhabitants, and in *Three Sisters*, in which the sisters are gradually evicted from their living space.

The endangered estate, in Chekhov's early plans, was to belong to a liberal-minded old lady who dressed like a girl, smoked, and couldn't do without society, a sympathetic sort tailored to the Maly Theatre's Olga Sadovskaya, who specialized in biddies and beldams. When the Maly Theatre refused to release her, Chekhov reshaped the role until it was suitable for someone of Olga Knipper's age. Only then did he conceive of Lopakhin. Varya first appeared as a grotesquely comic name, Varvara Nedotyopina (Varvara Left-in-the-Lurch): *Nedotyopa* eventually became the catchphrase of old Firs.

As Chekhov's letters reveal, he stressed the play's comic nature, and was put out when the Moscow Art Theatre saw it as a tearful tragedy. Even if some of Chekhov's complaints can be dismissed as a side effect of his physical deterioration, there is no doubt that the Art Theatre misplaced many of his intended emphases. He seems to have meant the major role to be the peasant-turned-millionaire Lopakhin, played by Stanislavsky. However, Stanislavsky, a millionaire of peasant origins, preferred the part of the feckless aristocrat Gaev, and handed Lopakhin over to Leonid Leonidov, a less experienced actor. Olga Knipper, whom the author saw in the grotesque role of the German governess, was cast as the elegant Ranevskaya. Immediately the central focus shifted to the genteel family of landowners, because the strongest actors were in those parts. Later on, fugitives from the Revolution identified so closely with Ranevskaya and Gaev that they disseminated a nostalgic view of the gentry's plight throughout the West. Soviet productions then went to the opposite extreme, reinterpreting Lopakhin as a man of the people capable of building a progressive society, and the student Trofimov as an eloquent harbinger of that brave new world.

Choosing sides immediately reduces the play's complexity and ambiguity. Chekhov had no axe to grind, not even the one that chops down the orchard. Neither Lopakhin nor Trofimov is invested with greater validity than Ranevskaya or Gaev. Trofimov is constantly undercut by comic devices: After a melodramatic exit line, "All is over between us," he falls downstairs, and, despite his claim to be in the vanguard of progress, is too absentminded to locate his own galoshes. Even his earnest speech about the idle upper classes and the benighted workers is addressed to the wrong audience: How can Ranevskaya possibly identify with the Asiatic bestiality that Trofimov indicts as a Russian characteristic? Only in the hearing of infatuated Anya do Trofimov's words seem prophetic; at other times, his inability to realize his situation renders them absurd.

Chekhov was anxious to avoid the stage clichés of the *kulak*, the hard-hearted, hard-fisted, loudmouthed merchant, in his portrayal of Lopakhin; after all, Lopakhin shares Chekhov's own background as a man of peasant origins who worked his way up in a closed society. He can be the tactless boor that Gaev insists he is, exulting over his purchase of the orchard and starting its decimation even before the family leaves. But, in the same breath, he is aware of his shortcomings, longs for a more poetic existence, and has, in the words of his antagonist Trofimov, "delicate, gentle fingers, like an artist . . . a delicate, gentle soul." And for all his pragmatism, he too is comically inept when it comes to romance. His halfhearted wooing of Varya may result from a more deep-seated love of her foster mother.

Ironically, it is the impractical Ranevskaya who pricks Lopakhin's dreams of giants and vast horizons and suggests that he examine his own gray life rather than build castles in the air. She may be an incorrigible romantic about the orchard and totally scatterbrained about money, but on matters of sex she is more clear-sighted than Lopakhin, Trofimov, or Gaev, who considers her "depraved." Prudish as a young Komsomol, Trofimov is scandalized by her advice that he take a mistress; he had been annoyed that Varya should distrust his moments alone with Anya.

In short, any attempt to grade Chekhov's characters as "right-thinking" or "wrong-headed" ignores the multifaceted nature of their portrayal. It would be a mistake to adopt wholeheartedly either the sentimental attitude of Gaev and Ranevskaya to the orchard or the pragmatic and "socially responsible" attitude of Lopakhin and Trofimov. By 1900 there were many works about uprooted gentlefolk and estates confiscated by *arrivistes*. Pyotr Nevezhin's *Second Youth* (1883), a popular melodrama dealing with the breakup of a nest of gentry, held the stage until the Revolution, and Chekhov had seen it. That same year Nikolay Solovyov's *Liquidation* appeared, in which an estate is saved by a rich peasant marrying the daughter of the family. Chekhov would not have been raking over these burnt-out themes if he did not have a fresh angle on them. *The Cherry Orchard* is the play in which Chekhov most successfully achieved a "new form," the amalgam of a symbolist outlook with the appurtenances of social comedy.

Perhaps the Russian critic A. R. Kugel was right when he wrote, "All the inhabitants of *The Cherry Orchard* are children and their behavior is childish."[1] Certainly, Chekhov seems to have abandoned his usual repertory company: There is no doctor, no mooning intellectual complaining of a wasted life (Yepikhodov may be a parody of that), no love triangles except the comic one of Yepikhodov-Dunyasha-Yasha. The only pistol is wielded by the hapless dolt Yepikhodov. Soliloquies have been replaced by monologues that are patently ridiculous (Gaev's speeches to the bookcase and the sunset) or misdirected (Trofimov's speech on progress). The absurdly named Simeonov-Pishchik, his "dear daughter Dashenka," and his rapid mood shifts would be out of place in *Three Sisters*. The upstart valet Yasha, who smells of chicken coops and cheap perfume, recalls Chichikov's servant Petrushka in *Dead Souls*, who permeates the ambience with his effluvium. Gogol, rather than Turgenev, is the presiding genius of this comedy.

All the characters are misfits, from Lopakhin, who dresses like a rich man but feels like a pig in a pastry shop, to Yasha and Dunyasha, servants who ape their betters, to the expelled student Trofimov, aimlessly hustled from place to place, to Yepikhodov, who puts simple ideas into inappropriate language, to Varya, who is an efficient manager but longs to be a pilgrim, to the most obvious example, the uprooted governess Charlotta, who has no notion who she is. Early on, we hear Lopakhin protest, "Got to remember who you are!" Jean-Louis Barrault, the French actor and director, suggested that the servants are satiric reflections of their

master's ideals:[2] Old Firs is the senile embodiment of the rosy
past Gaev waxes lyrical over; Yasha, that pushing young particle,
with his taste for Paris and champagne, is a parody of Lopakhin's
upward mobility and Ranevskaya's sophistication; Trofimov's
dreams of social betterment are mocked by Yepikhodov reading
Buckle and beefing up his vocabulary.

If there is a norm here, it exists offstage, in town, at the bank,
in the restaurant, in Mentone and Paris, where Ranevskaya's lover
entreats her return, or in Yaroslavl, where Great Aunt frowns on
the family's conduct. Chekhov peoples this unseen world with
what Vladimir Nabokov might call "homunculi." Besides the
lover and Auntie, there are Ranevskaya's alcoholic husband and
drowned son; Pishchik's daughter and the Englishmen who find
clay on his land; rich Deriganov, who might buy the estate; the
Ragulins, who hire Varya; the famous Jewish orchestra; Gaev's
deceased parents and servants; the staff, eating beans in the
kitchen; and a host of others to indicate that the cherry orchard is
a desert island in a teeming sea of life. The plethora of invisible
beings fortifies the sense of the estate's vulnerability, transience,
and isolation.

Barrault also pointed out that "the action" of the play is mea-
sured by the outside pressures on the estate. In Act One, the
cherry orchard is in danger of being sold, in Act Two it is on the
verge of being sold, in Act Three it is sold, and in Act Four it has
been sold. The characters are defined by their responses to these
"events," which, because they are spoken of, intuited, feared,
longed for, but never seen, automatically make the sale equiva-
lent to Fate or Death in a play of Maeterlinck or Andreev. As

Henri Bergson insisted,[3] any living being who tries to stand still in the evolving flow of time becomes mechanical and thus comical in action. How do the characters take a position in the temporal flow—are they delayed, do they move with it, do they try to outrun it? Those who refuse to join in (Gaev and Firs) or who rush to get ahead of it (Trofimov) can end up looking ridiculous.

Viewed as traditional comedy, *The Cherry Orchard* thwarts our expectations: The lovers are not threatened except by their own impotence, the servants are uppity but no help to anyone, all the characters are expelled at the end, but their personal habits have undergone no reformation. Ranevskaya returns to her lover; Gaev, at his most doleful moment, pops another candy in his mouth; Lopakhin and Trofimov are back on the road, one on business, the other on a mission. Even the abandonment of Firs hints that he cannot exist off the estate but is, as Ranevskaya's greeting to him implies, a piece of furniture like "my dear little table." This resilience in the face of change, with the future yet to be revealed, is closest to the symbolist sense of human beings trapped in the involuntary processes of time, their own mortality insignificant within the broader current. A Bergsonian awareness that reality stands outside time, dwarfing the characters' mundane concerns, imbues Chekhov's comedy with its bemused objectivity.

It also bestows on *The Cherry Orchard* its sense of persons suspended for the nonce. The present barely exists, elbowed aside by memory and nostalgia on the one hand and by expectation and hope on the other. When the play first opened, the critic M. Nevedomsky remarked that the characters are "living persons, painted with the colors of vivid reality, and at the same time schemata of that reality, as it were its foregone conclusions." Or as Kugel put it more succinctly, "the inhabitants of *The Cherry Orchard* live, as if half asleep, spectrally, on the border line of the real and the mystical."[4]

Chekhov's friend the writer Ivan Bunin pointed out that there were no such cherry orchards to be found in Russia, that Chekhov was inventing an imaginary landscape.[5] The estate is a wasteland in which the characters drift among the trivia of their lives while expecting something dire or important to occur. As in the symbolist dramas of the Belgian poet Maurice Maeterlinck, whom Chekhov admired, the play opens with two persons waiting in a dimly lit space, and closes with the imminent demise of a character abandoned in emptiness. Chekhov's favorite scenarios of waiting are especially attenuated here, since the suspense of "What will happen to the orchard?" dominates the first three acts, and in the last act the wait for carriages to arrive and effect the diaspora frames the conclusion.

However, the symbolism goes hand-in-glove with carefully observed reality; they coexist. Hence the uneasiness caused by what seem to be humdrum characters or situations. Act Two, with its open-air setting, demonstrates this concurrence of reality and super-reality. Chekhov's people are seldom at ease in the open. By removing the characters in *The Cherry Orchard* from the memory-laden atmosphere of the nursery (where children should feel at home), Chekhov strips them of their habitual defenses. In Act Two the characters meet on a road, one of those indeterminate locations, halfway between the railway station and the house but, symbolically, halfway between past and future, birth and death, being and nothingness. Something here impels them to deliver their innermost thoughts in monologues: Charlotta complains of her lack of identity, Yepikhodov declares his suicidal urges, Ranevskaya describes her "sinful" past, Gaev addresses the sunset, Trofimov speechifies about what's wrong with society, Lopakhin paints his hopes for Russia. As if hypnotized by the sound of their voices reverberating in the wilderness, they deliver up quintessences of themselves.

At this point comes the portentous moment of the snapped string. The moment is framed by those pauses that evoke the gaps in existence that Andrey Bely claimed were horrifying and that Beckett was to characterize as the transitional zone in which being made itself heard. Chekhov's characters again recall Maeterlinck's, faintly trying to surmise the nature of the potent force that hovers just outside the picture. The thought-filled pause, then the uncanny sound and the ensuing pause conjure up what lies beyond.

Even then, however, Chekhov does not forgo a realistic prextext for the inexplicable. Shortly before the moment, Yepikhodov crosses upstage, strumming his guitar. Might not the snapped string be one broken by the clumsy bookkeeper? At the play's end, before we hear the sound plangently dying away, we are told by Lopakhin that he has left Yepikhodov on the grounds as a caretaker. Chekhov always overlays any symbolic inference with a patina of irreproachable reality.

The party scene in Act Three is the supreme example of Chekhov's intermingling of subliminal symbol and surface reality. Bely saw it as a "crystallization of Chekhov's devices." It so struck the imagination of the young director Meyerhold that he wrote to Chekhov, on May 8, 1904, that "the play is abstract like a symphony by Chaikovsky . . . in [the party scene] there is something Maeterlinckian, terrifying." He later referred to "this nightmarish dance of puppets in a farce" in "Chekhov's new mystical drama."[6]

The act takes place in three dimensions: the forestage, with its brief interchanges by individual characters, the forced gaiety of the dancing in the background, and the offstage auction whose outcome looms over it all. Without leaving the sphere of the mundane, we have what Novalis called "a sequence of ideal events running parallel to reality." Characters are thrust out from the indistinct background and then return to it. Scantily identified, the postal clerk and the stationmaster surge forward, unaware of the main characters' inner lives, and make unwitting ironic comment. The stationmaster recites Aleksey Tolstoy's orotund poem, "The Sinful Woman," about a courtesan's conversion by Christ at a lavish orgy in Judaea. The opening lines, describing a sumptuous banquet, cast a sardonic reflection on the frumps gathered on this dismal occasion. They also show the earlier interview between the puritanical Trofimov and the self-confessed sinner Ranevskaya to be a parodic confrontation between a Messiah in eyeglasses and a Magdalene in a Parisian ballgown. The act culminates in the moving juxtaposition of Ranevskaya's weeping and Lopakhin's laughter, as the unseen musicians play loudly at his behest.

The return to the nursery, now stripped of its evocative trappings, in Act Four, confirms the inexorable expulsion. In Act One, it has been a room to linger in; now it is a cheerless space in which characters loiter only momentarily on their way to somewhere else. The old Russian tradition of sitting for a moment before taking leave becomes especially meaningful when there are no chairs, only trunks and bundles to perch on. The ghosts that Gaev and Ranevskaya had seen in the orchard in the first act have now moved indoors, in the person of Firs, who is doomed to haunt the scene of the past, since he has no future.

The consummate mastery of *The Cherry Orchard* is revealed in an authorial shorthand that is both impressionistic and theatrical. The pull on Ranevskaya to return to Paris takes shape in the telegram prop: In Act One, she tears up the telegrams; by Act Three, she has preserved them in her handbag; in Act Four, the lodestones draw her back. The dialogue is similarly telegraphic, as in Anya's short speech about her mother's flat in Paris. "Mama is living on the sixth floor, I walk all the way up, there are some French people there, ladies, an old Catholic priest with a pamphlet, and it's full of cigarette smoke, not nice at all." In a few strokes, a past is encapsulated: a high walk-up (signifying Ranevskaya's reduced circumstances), her toying with religious conversion, a *louche* atmosphere.

Each character is distinguished by an appropriate speech pattern. Ranevskaya constantly employs diminutives and terms of endearment; for her everyone is *golubchik*, "dovey." She is also vague, using adjectives like "some kind of" (*kakoy-to*). Gaev is a parody of the after-dinner speaker: Emotion can be voiced only in fulsome oration, thick with platitudes. When his flow is stanched, he falls back on billiard terms or stops his mouth with candy and anchovies. Pishchik has high blood pressure, so Chekhov the doctor makes sure he speaks in short, breathless phrases, a hodgepodge of old-world courtesy, hunting terms, and newspaper talk. Lopakhin's language is more varied, according to his interlocutor: blunt and colloquial with servants, more respectful with his former betters. As suits a businessman, he speaks concisely and in well-structured sentences, citing exact numbers and a commercial vocabulary, with frequent glances at his watch. Only in dealing with Varya does he resort to ponderous facetiousness and even bleating.

Memorably, Firs's "half-baked bungler" is the last line in the play. Its periodic repetition suggests that Chekhov meant it to sum up all the characters. They are all inchoate, some, like Anya and Trofimov, in the process of taking shape, others, like Gaev and Yepikhodov, never to take shape. The whole play has been held in a similar state of contingency until the final moments, when real chopping begins in the orchard and, typically, it is heard from offstage, mingled with the more cryptic and reverberant sound of the snapped string.

NOTES

1 A. R. Kugel, *Russkie dramaturgi* (Moscow: Mir, 1934), p. 120.

2 Jean-Louis Barrault, "*Pourquoi La Cerisaie?*," *Cahiers de la Compagnie Barrault-Renaud* 6 (July 1954): 87–97.

3 Henri Bergson, *Laughter: An Essay on the Meaning of the Comic*, trans. Cloudesley Brereton and Fred Rothwell (New York: Macmillan, 1911), pp. 88–89.

4 M. Nevedomsky, "Simvolizm v posledney drame A. P. Chekhova," *Mir bozhy* 8, 2 (1904): 18–19. Kugel, op. cit., p. 125.

5 Ivan Bunin, *O Chekhove* (New York: Chekhov Publishing House, 1955), p. 216.

6 Andrey Bely, "Vishnyovy sad," *Vesy* (*Balances*) 5 (1904); Vsevolod Meyerhold, *Perepiska* (Moscow: Iskusstvo, 1976), p. 45; and "Teatr (k istorii tekhnike)," in (St. Petersburg: Shipovnik, 1908), pp. 143–145.

THE CHERRY ORCHARD[1]

Вишнёвый Сад

A Comedy[2]

CHARACTERS[3]

RANEVSKAYA, LYUBOV ANDREEVNA, *a landowner*

ANYA, *her daughter, 17*

VARYA, *her foster daughter, 24*

---

1 According to Stanislavsky, Chekhov wavered between the pronunciations *Vishnevy sad* (accentuated on the first syllable, "an orchard of cherries") and *Vishnyovy sad* (accentuated on the second syllable, "a cherry orchard"). He decided on the latter. "The former is a market garden, a plantation of cherry-trees, a profitable orchard which still had value. But the latter offers no profit, it does nothing but preserve within itself and its snow-white blossoms the poetry of the life of the masters of olden times" (*My Life in Art*).

2 This subtitle was used in the Marks edition of 1904. On the posters and publicity the play was denominated a drama.

3 To a Russian ear, certain associations can be made with the names. Lyubov means love, and a kind of indiscriminate love characterizes Ranevskaya. Gaev suggests *gaer*, buffoon, while Lopakhin may be derived from either *lopata*, shovel, or *lopat*, to shovel food down one's gullet—both earthy-sounding. Simeonov-Pishchik combines an ancient autocratic name with a silly one reminiscent of *pishchat*, to chirp, something like De Montfort-Tweet. A *pishchik* is a "swozzle," or pipe, used by puppeteers to produce the voice of Petrushka, the Russian Punch.

GAEV, LEONID ANDREEVICH, *Ranevskaya's brother*

LOPAKHIN, YERMOLAY ALEKSEICH, *a businessman*

TROFIMOV, PYOTR SERGEEVICH, *a university student*

SIMEONOV-PISHCHIK, BORIS BORISOVICH, *a landowner*

CHARLOTTA IVANOVA, *a governess*

YEPIKHODOV, SEMYON PANTELEEVICH, *a bookkeeper*

DUNYASHA, *a parlor maid*

FIRS[4] NIKOLAEVICH, *a valet, an old-timer of 87*

YASHA, *a young valet*

A VAGRANT

THE STATION MASTER

A POSTAL CLERK

GUESTS, SERVANTS

---

4 He is named for the Orthodox Saint Thyrsus (martyred 251).

*The action takes place on Ranevskaya's
country estate.*[5]

ACT ONE

*A room, which is still known as the nursery. One of
the doors opens into Anya's bedroom. Dawn, soon
the sun will be up. It is already May, the cherry trees
are in bloom, but it is chilly in the orchard, there
is an early morning frost. The windows in the room
are shut. Enter DUNYASHA carrying a candle and
LOPAKHIN holding a book.*

LOPAKHIN. Train's pulled in, thank God. What time is it?

DUNYASHA. Almost two. (*Blows out the candle.*) Light already.

LOPAKHIN. But just how late was the train? A couple of hours at
least. (*Yawns and stretches.*) That's me all over, had to do something stupid! Drove over here on purpose, to meet them at the

---

5 "It's an old manor house: once the life in it was very opulent, and this must be felt
in the furnishings. Opulent and comfortable" (Chekhov to Olga Knipper, October 14,
1903). "The house in the play has two stories, is big. After all, in Act Three, there's talk
about 'down the stairs' " (to Stanislavsky, November 5, 1903). Stanislavsky decided that
the estate was located in the Oryol province near Kursk, possibly because the area is
rich in potter's clay and would justify the Englishmen in Act Four finding "some sort
of white clay" on Pishchik's land.

station, and spent the time fast asleep . . . Sat down and dropped off. Annoying . . . Though you should have woke me up.

DUNYASHA. I thought you'd gone. (*Listening.*) There, sounds like they're driving up.

LOPAKHIN (*listening*). No . . . the luggage has to be loaded, one thing and another . . . (*Pause.*) Lyubov Andreevna's been living abroad five years now, I don't know what she's like these days . . . A good sort of person, that's her. A kind-hearted, unpretentious person. I remember, when I was just a kid about fifteen,[6] my late father—he kept a shop in this village back then—punched me in the face with his fist, blood was gushing from my nose . . . We'd come into the yard back then for some reason, and he'd been drinking. Lyubov Andreevna, I remember as though it was yesterday, still a youngish lady, so slender, brought me to the washstand, here in this very room, the nursery. "Don't cry," she says, "my little peasant, you'll live long enough to get married . . ."

Pause.

My little peasant . . . My father, true, was a peasant, and here I am in a white waistcoat, yellow high-button shoes. Like a pig's snout on a tray of pastry . . .[7] Only difference is I'm rich, plenty

---

6 In an earlier version, the boy's age was five or six. At that time Chekhov still saw Ranevskaya as an old woman. He reduced her age when it became clear that Olga Knipper would play the part.

7 Literally, "with a pig's snout in White-Bread Row," the street in any city market where fine baked goods are sold.

of money, but if you think it over and work it out, once a peasant, always a peasant . . .[8] (*Leafs through the book.*) I was reading this here book and couldn't make head or tail of it. Reading and nodding off.

Pause.

DUNYASHA. The dogs didn't sleep all night, they can sense the mistress is coming home.

LOPAKHIN. What's got into you, Dunyasha, you're so . . .

DUNYASHA. My hands are trembling. I'm going to swoon.

LOPAKHIN. Much too delicate, that's what you are, Dunyasha. Dressing up like a young lady, fixing your hair like one too. Mustn't do that. Got to remember who you are.

---

8 "Lopakhin must be not be played as a loudmouth, that isn't the invariable sign of a merchant. He's a suave man" (Chekhov to Olga Knipper, October 30, 1903). "Lopakhin is a merchant, true; but a very decent person in every respect; he must behave with perfect decorum, like an educated man with no petty ways or tricks . . . In casting an actor in the part, you must remember that Varya, a serious and religious young girl, is in love with Lopakhin: she wouldn't be in love with some little moneygrubber . . ." (Chekhov to Stanislavsky, October 30, 1903). "Lopakhin—a white waistcoat and yellow high-button shoes; walks swinging his arms, a broad stride, thinks while walking, walks a straight line. Hair not short, and therefore often tosses back his head, while in thought he combs his beard, back to front, i.e., from his neck toward his mouth" (Chekhov to Nemirovich-Danchenko, November 2, 1903).

According to L. M. Leonidov,

[Chekhov] told me that Lopakhin outwardly should either be like a merchant or like a medical professor at Moscow University. And later, at the rehearsals, after Act Three he said to me:

"Listen, Lopakhin doesn't shout. He is rich, and rich men never shout." . . .

When I inquired of Chekhov how to play Lopakhin, he replied: "In yellow high-button shoes."

("Past and Present," *Moscow Art Theatre Yearbook for 1944*, vol. 1 [1946])

YEPIKHODOV[9] *enters with a bouquet; he is wearing*
a jacket and brightly polished boots, which squeak
noisily. On entering, he drops the bouquet.

YEPIKHODOV (*picks up the bouquet*). Here, the gardener sent them, he says stick 'em in the dining room. (*He hands Dunyasha the bouquet.*)

LOPAKHIN. And bring me some kvas.[10]

DUNYASHA. Yes, sir. (*Exits.*)

YEPIKHODOV. There's a morning frost now, three degrees below, but the cherries are all in bloom. I can't condone our climate. (*Sighs.*) I can't. Our climate cannot be conducive in the right way. Look, Yermolay Alekseich, if I might append, day before yesterday I bought myself some boots and they, I venture to assure you, squeak so loud, it's quite out of the question. What's the best kind of grease?

---

9 A parody of the self-made man represented by Lopakhin. Chekhov first envisaged the character as plump and elderly, but revised this to fit one of his favorite actors, Ivan Moskvin, who was young and trim. The character had several originals. Yepikhodov's autodidacticism, reading abstruse books to better his mind, originated when Chekhov suggested to one of his attendants in Yalta that he go in for self-improvement. So the man went out, bought a red tie, and announced his intention of learning French. Yepikhodov's clumsiness derives from a conjuring clown Chekhov saw perform at the Hermitage gardens. The act consisted of disasters: juggled eggs smashing on the clown's forehead, dishes crashing to the ground, while the woebegone wizard stood with an expression of bewilderment and embarrassment. Chekhov kept shouting, "Wonderful! It's wonderful!" (Stanislavsky, *Teatralnaya gazeta*, November 27, 1914).

10 A refreshing drink of low alcohol content, made from fermented black bread and malt, much preferred to beer by the peasantry.

LOPAKHIN. Leave me alone. You wear me out.

YEPIKHODOV. Every day I experience some kind of hard luck. But I don't complain, I'm used to it. I even smile.

DUNYASHA enters and gives Lopakhin a glass of kvas.[11]

YEPIKHODOV. I'm on my way. (*Bumps into a chair, which falls over.*) Look . . . (*As if in triumph.*) There, you see, pardon the expression, what a circumstance, one of many . . ∴. It's simply incredible! (*He exits.*)

DUNYASHA. I have to confess, Yermolay Alekseich, Yepikhodov proposed to me.

YEPIKHODOV. Ah!

DUNYASHA. I don't know how to handle it . . . He's a quiet sort, but sometimes he just starts talking, and you can't understand a word. It's nice and it's sensitive, only you can't understand a word. I kind of like him. He's madly in love with me. As a person he's always in trouble, something goes wrong every day. So around here we've taken to calling him Tons of Trouble . . .[12]

LOPAKHIN (*hearkening*). Listen, I think they're coming . . .

---

11 "Dunya and Yepikhodov stand in Lopakhin's presence, they do not sit. Lopakhin, after all, deports himself freely, like a lord, uses the familiar form in speaking to the housemaid, whereas she uses the formal form to him" (Chekhov to Stanislavsky, November 10, 1903).

12 Literally, *Dvadtsat-dva neschastye*, Twenty-two Misfortunes, "twenty-two" being a number indicating "lots." *Neschastye* is a recurrent word throughout the play.

DUNYASHA. They're coming! What's the matter with me . . . I've got cold chills.

LOPAKHIN. They're coming. Let's go meet them. Will she recognize me? It's five years since last we met.

DUNYASHA (*flustered*). I'll faint this minute . . . Ah, I'll faint!

We hear the sound of two carriages drawing up to the house. LOPAKHIN and DUNYASHA go out quickly. The stage is empty. Noise begins in the adjoining rooms. FIRS, leaning on a stick, hurries across the stage; he has just been to meet Lyubov Andreevna; he is wearing an old suit of livery and a top hat; he mutters something to himself, but no words can be made out. A voice: "Let's go through here." LYUBOV ANDREEVNA,[13] ANYA, and CHARLOTTA IVANOVNA with a lapdog on a leash, all three dressed in traveling clothes, VARYA in an overcoat and kerchief, GAEV, SIMEONOV-PISHCHIK, LOPAKHIN, DUNYASHA with a bundle and parasol, SERVANTS carrying suitcases—all pass through the room.

13 "No, I never wanted to suggest that Ranevskaya is chastened. The only thing that can chasten a woman like that is death . . . It isn't hard to play Ranevskaya; you only need from the beginning to take the right tone; you need to come up with a smile and a way of laughing, you have to know how to dress" (Chekhov to Olga Knipper, October 25, 1903).

ANYA.[14] Let's go through here. Mama, do you remember what room this is?

LYUBOV ANDREEVNA (*joyfully, through tears*). The nursery!

VARYA. It's cold, my hands are numb. (*To Lyubov Andreevna.*) Your rooms, the white and the violet, are still the same as ever, Mama dear.

LYUBOV ANDREEVNA. The nursery, my darling, beautiful room . . . I slept here when I was a little girl . . . (*Weeps.*) And now I feel like a little girl . . . (*She kisses her brother and Varya and then her brother again.*) And Varya is just the same as ever, looks like a nun. And I recognized Dunyasha . . . (*Kisses Dunyasha.*)

GAEV. The train was two hours late. What'd y' call that? What kind of system is that?

CHARLOTTA (*to Pishchik*). My dog eats nuts even.[15]

---

14 "Anya [is] a bobtailed, uninteresting role. Varya [. . .] is a little nun, a little silly" (Chekhov to Nemirovich-Danchenko, October 30, 1903). "Anya can be played by anybody you like, even by an altogether unknown actress, only she must be young and look like a little girl, and talk in a young, ringing voice. This is not one of the major roles. Varya is a more important role . . . Varya does not resemble Sonya and Natasha; she is a figure in a black dress, a little nun, a little silly, a crybaby, etc., etc." (Chekhov to Nemirovich-Danchenko, November 2 , 1903).

15 "Charlotta is a major role . . . Charlotta speaks correct, not broken, Russian, but occasionally she pronounces the soft ending of a word hard, and she confuses the masculine and feminine gender of adjectives" (Chekhov to Nemirovich-Danchenko, November 2, 1903).

"Muratova, who played Charlotta, asks Anton Pavlovich, might she wear a green necktie.

"'You may but it's not necessary,' the author answers" (L. M. Leonidov, "Past and

PISHCHIK (*astounded*).[16] Can you imagine!

They all go out, except for ANYA and DUNYASHA.

DUNYASHA. We're worn out with waiting . . . (*Helps Anya out of her overcoat and hat.*)

ANYA. I couldn't sleep the four nights on the train . . . now I'm so frozen.

DUNYASHA. You left during Lent, there was snow then too, frost, and now? My darling! (*She laughs and kisses her.*) We're worn out with waiting for you, my pride and joy . . . I'll tell you now, I can't hold it back another minute . . .

ANYA (*weary*). Always something . . .

DUNYASHA. Yepikhodov the bookkeeper right after Easter proposed to me.

ANYA. You've got a one-track mind . . . (*Setting her hair to rights.*) I've lost all my hair pins . . . (*She is very tired, practically staggering.*)

DUNYASHA. I just don't know what to think. He loves me, loves me so much!

Present," *Moscow Art Theatre Yearbook for 1944*, vol. 1 [1946]).

The character was based on an eccentric English governess, whom Chekhov had met while staying on Stanislavsky's estate. This acrobatic Miss Prism would leap up on Chekhov's shoulders and salute passersby by taking off his hat and forcing him to bow (*My Life in Art*, Russian ed.).

16 "Pishchik is a real Russian, an old man, debilitated by gout, old age, and over-indulgence, stout, dressed in a tight, long-waisted frockcoat . . . , boots without heels" (Chekhov to Nemirovich-Danchenko, November 2, 1903).

ANYA (*peering through the door to her room, tenderly*). My room, my windows, as if I'd never gone away. I'm home! Tomorrow morning I'll get up, run through the orchard . . . Oh, if only I could get some sleep! I couldn't sleep the whole way, I was worried to death.

DUNYASHA. Day before yesterday, Pyotr Sergeich arrived.

ANYA (*joyfully*). Petya!

DUNYASHA. The gent's sleeping in the bathhouse, the gent's staying there. "I'm afraid," says the gent, "to be a nuisance." (*Looking at her pocket watch.*) Somebody ought to wake the gent up, but Varvara Mikhailovna gave the order not to. "Don't you wake him up," she says.

    Enter VARYA, *with a key ring on her belt.*

VARYA. Dunyasha, coffee right away . . . Mama dear is asking for coffee.

DUNYASHA. Just a minute. (*She exits.*)

VARYA. Well, thank God you're here. You're home again. (*Caressing her.*) My darling's here again! My beauty's here again!

ANYA. What I've been through.

VARYA. I can imagine!

ANYA. I left during Holy Week, it was so cold then. Charlotta kept talking the whole way, doing tricks. Why you stuck me with Charlotta . . .

VARYA. You couldn't have traveled by yourself, precious. Seventeen years old!

ANYA. We get to Paris, it was cold there too, snowing. My French is awful. Mama is living on the sixth floor, I walk all the way up, there are some French people there, ladies, an old Catholic priest with a pamphlet, and it's full of cigarette smoke, not nice at all. And suddenly I started to feel sorry for Mama, so sorry for her, I took her head in my hands and couldn't let go. Then Mama kept hugging me, crying . . .

VARYA (*through tears*). Don't talk about it, don't talk about it . . .

ANYA. The villa near Mentone[17] she'd already sold, she had nothing left, nothing. And I hadn't a kopek left either, we barely got this far. And Mama doesn't understand! We sit down to dinner at a station, and she orders the most expensive meal and gives each waiter a ruble tip. Charlotta's the same. Yasha insists on his share too, it's simply awful. Of course Mama has a manservant, Yasha, we brought him back.

VARYA. I saw the low-life . . .

ANYA. Well, how are things? Have we paid the interest?

VARYA. What with?

ANYA. Oh dear, oh dear . . .

_____

17 Or Menton, a resort area on the Mediterranean coast of France. Nearby lies Monte Carlo, another suggestion of Ranevskaya's extravagance.

VARYA. In August the estate's to be auctioned off . . .

ANYA. Oh dear . . .

LOPAKHIN (*sticking his head in the doorway and bleating*). Me-e-eh . . . (*Exits.*)

VARYA (*through tears*). I'd like to smack him one . . . (*Shakes her fist.*)

ANYA (*embraces Varya, quietly*). Varya, has he proposed? (*VARYA shakes her head no.*) He *does* love you . . . Why don't you talk it over, what are you waiting for?

VARYA. I don't think it will work out for us. He has so much business, can't get around to me . . . and he pays me no mind. Forget about him, I can't stand to look at him . . . Everybody talks about our getting married, everybody says congratulations, but as a matter of fact, there's nothing to it, it's all like a dream . . . (*In a different tone.*) You've got a brooch like a bumblebee.

ANYA (*sadly*). Mama bought it. (*Goes to her room, speaks cheerfully, like a child.*) And in Paris I went up in a balloon!

VARYA. My darling's here again! My beauty's here again!

DUNYASHA has returned with a coffeepot and is brewing coffee.

(*Stands near the door.*) The whole day long, darling, while

I'm doing my chores, I keep dreaming. If only there were a rich man for you to marry, even I would be at peace, I'd go to a hermitage, then to Kiev . . . to Moscow, and I'd keep on going like that to holy shrines . . . I'd go on and on. Heaven! . . .[18]

ANYA. The birds are singing in the orchard. What time is it now?

VARYA. Must be three. Time for you to be asleep, dearest. (*Going into Anya's room.*) Heaven!

YASHA enters with a lap rug and a traveling bag.

YASHA (*crosses the stage; in a refined way*). May I come through, ma'am?

DUNYASHA. A person wouldn't recognize you, Yasha. You've really changed abroad.

YASHA. Mm . . . who are you?

DUNYASHA. When you left here, I was so high . . . (*Measures from the floor.*) Dunyasha, Fyodor Kozoedov's daughter. You don't remember!

YASHA. Mm . . . Tasty little pickle! (*Glances around and embraces her, she shrieks and drops a saucer. YASHA exits hurriedly.*)

---

18 Becoming a *bogomolets*, or pilgrim, was a common avocation in pre-Revolutionary Russia, especially for the rootless and outcast. One would trek from shrine to shrine, putting up at monasteries and living off alms. Varya's picture of such a life is highly idealized. Its picaresque side can be glimpsed in Nikolay Leskov's stories, such as "The Enchanted Pilgrim," in the ambiguous figure Luka in Gorky's 1902 play *The Lower Depths,* and in Chekhov's *Along the Highway.*

VARYA (*in the doorway, crossly*). Now what was that?

DUNYASHA (*through tears*). I broke a saucer . . .

VARYA. That's good luck.

ANYA (*entering from her room*). We ought to warn Mama that Petya's here . . .

VARYA. I gave orders not to wake him.

ANYA (*thoughtfully*). Six years ago father died, a month later our brother Grisha drowned in the river, a sweet little boy, seven years old. Mama couldn't stand it, she went away, went away without looking back . . . (*Shivers.*) How well I understand her, if only she knew!

Pause.

Since Petya Trofimov was Grisha's tutor, he might remind her . . .

Enter FIRS in a jacket and white waistcoat.

FIRS (*goes to the coffeepot; preoccupied*). The mistress will take it in here . . . (*Putting on white gloves.*) Cawrfee ready? (*Sternly to Dunyasha.*) You! What about cream?

DUNYASHA. Oh, my goodness . . . (*Exits hurriedly.*)

FIRS (*fussing with the coffeepot*). Eh you, half-baked bun-gler[19] . . . (*Mumbles to himself.*) Come home from Paris . . .

---

19 *Nedotyopa* was not a Russian word when Chekhov used it; it was Ukrainian for an incompetent, a mental defective. Chekhov may have remembered hearing it in his

And the master went to Paris once upon a time . . . by coach
and horses . . . (*Laughs.*)

VARYA. Firs, what are you on about?

FIRS. What's wanted, miss? (*Joyfully.*) My mistress has come
home! I've been waiting! Now I can die . . . (*Weeps with joy.*)

Enter LYUBOV ANDREEVNA, GAEV,
LOPAKHIN, and SIMEONOV-PISHCHIK, the last
in a long-waisted coat of expensive cloth and baggy
pantaloons.[20] *GAEV, on entering, moves his arms and*
torso as if he were playing billiards.

LYUBOV ANDREEVNA. How does it go? Let me remember . . . Yellow in the corner! Doublette in the center![21]

---

childhood; it does not appear in Russian dictionaries until 1938, and then Chekhov is
cited as the source. George Calderon perceived the etymology to derive from *ne*, not,
and *dotyapat*, to finish chopping, which makes great sense in the context of the play.
Translators grow gray over the word: earlier English versions have "good-for-nothing,"
"rogue," "duffer," "job-lot," "lummox," "silly young cuckoo," "silly old nothing," "nin-
compoop," "muddler," "silly galoot," "numbskull," "young flibbertigibbet." The critic
Batyushkov considered the whole play to be a variation on the theme of "nedotyopery,"
each of the characters representing a different aspect of life unfulfilled.

20 Pishchik's costume makes him look more traditionally Russian than the others:
the long coat and baggy pants tucked into boots are modern adaptations of medieval
boyar dress.

21 In pre-Revolutionary Russia, billiards was played with five balls, one of them yellow. A doublette occurs when a player's ball hits the cushion, rebounds, and sinks the
other player's ball. George Calderon ventured that Gaev "always plays a declaration
game at billiards, no flukes allowed." Chekhov asked the actor he wanted to play Gaev
to brush up on the terminology and add the proper phrases in rehearsal. "Ask Vishnevsky to listen in on people playing billiards and jot down as many billiard terms as he
can. I don't play billiards, or did once, but now I've forgotten it all, and stick them in

GAEV. Red in the corner! Once upon a time, sister, we used to sleep together here in this room, and now I've turned fifty-one, strange as it seems . . .

LOPAKHIN. Yes, time marches on.

GAEV. How's that?[22]

LOPAKHIN. Time, I say, marches on.

GAEV. It smells of cheap perfume[23] in here.

ANYA. I'm going to bed. Good night, Mama. (*Kisses her mother.*)

LYUBOV ANDREEVNA. My dazzling little princess.[24] (*Kisses her hands.*) Are you glad you're home? I can't get over it.

ANYA. Good night, Uncle.

GAEV (*kisses her face, hands*). God bless you. How like your mother you are! (*To his sister.*) Lyuba, at her age you were just the same.

> ANYA *gives her hand to Lopakhin and Pishchik, exits,*
> *and shuts the door behind her.*

---

my play any old way. Later on Vishnevsky and I will talk it over, and I'll write in what's needed" (Chekhov to Olga Knipper, October 14, 1903).

22 The colloquial "*Kogo*" (literally, "Whom?") instead of "*chego*" ("What's that?"), the quirky locution of an aristocrat.

23 Patchouli, an oil made from an Asian plant, which has a very powerful aroma, prized in the Orient, but insufferable to many Westerners.

24 *Nenaglyadnaya ditsyusya moya*, literally, "blindingly beauteous bairn of mine," a formula found in fairy tales.

LYUBOV ANDREEVNA. She's utterly exhausted.

PISHCHIK. Must be a long trip.

VARYA (*to Lopakhin and Pishchik*). Well, gentlemen? Three o'clock, by this time you've worn out your welcome.

LYUBOV ANDREEVNA (*laughing*). And you're still the same too, Varya. (*Draws Varya to her and kisses her.*) First I'll have some coffee, then everybody will go.

FIRS puts a cushion under her feet.

Thank you, dear. I've grown accustomed to coffee. I drink it night and day. Thank you, my old dear. (*Kisses Firs.*)

VARYA. I've got to see if all the luggage was brought in . . . (*Exits.*)

LYUBOV ANDREEVNA. Can I really be sitting here? (*Laughs.*) I feel like jumping up and down and swinging my arms. (*Covers her face with her hands.*) But suppose I'm dreaming! God knows, I love my country, love it dearly, I couldn't look at it from the train, couldn't stop crying. (*Through tears.*) However, we should have some coffee. Thank you, Firs, thank you, my old dear. I'm so glad you're still alive.

FIRS. Day before yesterday.

GAEV. He's hard of hearing.

LOPAKHIN. I've got to leave for Kharkov right away, around five. What a nuisance! I wanted to feast my eyes on you, have a chat . . . You're still as lovely as ever.

PISHCHIK (*breathing hard*). Even prettier . . . Dressed in Parisian fashions . . . "lost my cart with all four wheels . . ."[25]

LOPAKHIN. Your brother, Leonid Andreich here, says that I'm an oaf, I'm a money-grubbing peasant,[26] but it doesn't make the least bit of difference to me. Let him talk. The only thing I want is for you to believe in me as you once did, for your wonderful, heartbreaking eyes to look at me as they once did. Merciful God! My father was your grandfather's serf, and your father's, but you, you personally did so much for me once that I forgot all that and love you like my own kin . . . more than my own kin.

LYUBOV ANDREEVNA. I can't sit still, I just can't . . . (*Leaps up and walks about in great excitement.*) I won't survive this joy . . . Laugh at me, I'm silly . . . My dear little cupboard. (*Kisses the cupboard.*) My little table.

GAEV. While you were away Nanny died.

LYUBOV ANDREEVNA (*sits and drinks coffee*). Yes, rest in peace. They wrote me.

GAEV. And Anastasy died. Cross-eyed Petrusha left me and now he's working in town for the chief of police. (*Takes a little box of hard candies out of his pocket and sucks one.*)

---

25 The rest of the folksong verse goes "lost my heart head over heels." It means "Going the whole hog."

26 *Kulak*, literally a fist, but figuratively a tight-fisted peasant or small dealer.

PISHCHIK. My dear daughter Dashenka . . . sends her regards . . .

LOPAKHIN. I'd like to tell you something you'd enjoy, something to cheer you up. (*Looking at his watch.*) I have to go
now, never time for a real conversation . . . well, here it is in a
nutshell. As you already know, the cherry orchard will be sold
to pay your debts, the auction is set for August twenty-second,
but don't you worry, dear lady, don't lose any sleep, there's a
way out . . . Here's my plan. Your attention, please! Your estate
lies only thirteen miles from town, the railroad runs past it,
and if the cherry orchard and the land along the river were
subdivided into building lots and then leased out for summer
cottages, you'd have an income of at the very least twenty-five
thousand a year.

GAEV. Excuse me, what rubbish!

LYUBOV ANDREEVNA. I don't quite follow you, Yermolay Alekseich.

LOPAKHIN. You'll get out of the summer tenants at least twenty-
five rubles a year for every two and a half acres, and if you
advertise now, I'll bet whatever you like that by fall there
won't be a single lot left vacant, they'll all be snapped up. In
short, congratulations, you're saved. The location's wonderful,
the river's deep. Only, of course, it'll have to be spruced up,
cleared out . . . for example, tear down all the old sheds, and
this house, say, which is absolutely worthless, chop down the
old cherry orchard . . .

LYUBOV ANDREEVNA. Chop it down? My dear, forgive me, but you don't understand at all. If there's anything of interest in the entire district, even outstanding, it's none other than our cherry orchard.[27]

LOPAKHIN. The only outstanding thing about this orchard is it's very big. The soil produces cherries every other year, and then there's no way to get rid of them, nobody buys them.

GAEV. The *Encyclopedia* makes reference to this orchard . . .

LOPAKHIN (*after a glance at his watch*). If we don't think up something and come to some decision, then on the twenty-second of August the cherry orchard and the whole estate will be sold at auction. Make up your mind! There's no other way out, I promise you. Absolutely none.

FIRS. In the old days, forty-fifty years back, cherries were dried, preserved, pickled, made into jam, and sometimes . . .

---

27 Chekhov's close friend, the writer Ivan Bunin, objected to this feature of the play. "I grew up in just such an impoverished 'nest of gentry,'" he wrote. "It was a desolate estate on the steppes, but with a large orchard, not cherry, of course, for, Chekhov to the contrary, nowhere in Russia were there orchards comprised *exclusively* of cherries; only *sections* of the orchards on these estates (though sometimes very vast sections) grew cherries, and nowhere, Chekhov to the contrary again, could these sections be *directly beside* the main house, nor was there anything wonderful about the cherry trees, which are quite unattractive, as everyone knows, gnarled with puny leaves, puny blossoms when in bloom (quite unlike those which blossom so enormously and lushly right under the very windows of the main house at the Art Theatre) . . ." (*O Chekhove* [New York, 1955], pp. 215–216).

GAEV. Be quiet, Firs.

FIRS. And used to be whole cartloads of dried cherries were sent to Moscow and Kharkov. Then there was money! And in those days the dried cherries were tender, juicy, sweet, tasty . . . They had a recipe then . . .

LYUBOV ANDREEVNA. And where's that recipe today?

FIRS. It's forgot. Nobody remembers.

PISHCHIK (*to Lyubov*). What's going on in Paris? What was it like? You eat frogs?

LYUBOV ANDREEVNA. I ate crocodiles.

PISHCHIK. Can you imagine . . .

LOPAKHIN. So far there's only been gentry and peasants in the country, but now there's these vacationers. Every town, even the smallest, is surrounded these days by summer cottages. And I'll bet that over the next twenty-odd years the summer vacationer will multiply fantastically. Now all he does is drink tea on his balcony, but it might just happen that on his two and a half acres he starts growing things, and then your cherry orchard will become happy, rich, lush . . .

GAEV (*getting indignant*). What drivel!

Enter VARYA and YASHA.

VARYA. Mama dear, there are two telegrams for you. (*Selects a key; with a jangle opens the antique cupboard.*) Here they are.

LYUBOV ANDREEVNA. They're from Paris. (*Tears up the telegrams without reading them.*) I'm through with Paris . . .

GAEV. Lyuba, do you know how old that cupboard is? A week ago I pulled out the bottom drawer, took a look, and there are numbers branded on it. This cupboard was built exactly one hundred years ago. How d'you like that? Eh? Maybe we ought to celebrate its centenary. An inanimate object, but all the same, any way you look at it, this cupboard is a repository for books.

PISHCHIK (*astounded*). A hundred years . . . Can you imagine!

GAEV. Yes . . . This thing . . . (*Stroking the cupboard.*) Dear, venerated cupboard! I salute your existence, which for over a century has been dedicated to enlightened ideals of virtue and justice; your unspoken appeal to constructive endeavor has not faltered in the course of a century, sustaining (*through tears*) in generations of our line, courage, faith in a better future and nurturing within us ideals of decency and social consciousness.[28]

Pause.

LOPAKHIN. Right . . .

LYUBOV ANDREEVNA. You're still the same, Lyonya.

---

28 Chekhov is making fun of the Russian mania for celebrating anniversaries. Stanislavsky reports that on the twenty-fifth anniversary of Chekhov's literary career, held during the third performance of *The Cherry Orchard*, "One of the men of letters began his speech of tribute with the same words that Gaev addresses to the old cupboard in Act One of *The Cherry Orchard*, 'Dear, venerated.' Only instead of cupboard, the orator said 'Anton Pavlovich.' Chekhov winked at me and smiled a wicked smile" (*Letters*).

GAEV (*somewhat embarrassed*). Carom to the right corner! Red in the center!

LOPAKHIN (*glancing at his watch*). Well, my time's up.

YASHA (*handing medicine to Lyubov*). Maybe you'll take your pills now . . .

PISHCHIK. Shouldn't take medicine, dearest lady . . . It does no good, or harm . . . Hand 'em over . . . most respected lady. (*He takes the pills, shakes them into his palm, blows on them, pops them into his mouth, and drinks some kvas.*) There!

LYUBOV ANDREEVNA (*alarmed*). You've gone crazy!

PISHCHIK. I took all the pills.

LOPAKHIN. He's a bottomless pit.

They all laugh.

FIRS. The gent stayed with us Holy Week, ate half a bucket of pickles . . . (*Mumbles.*)

LYUBOV ANDREEVNA. What is he on about?

VARYA. For three years now he's been mumbling like that. We're used to it.

YASHA. Second childhood.

*CHARLOTTA IVANOVNA crosses the stage in a
white dress. She is very slender, tightly laced, with a
pair of pince-nez on a cord at her waist.*

LOPAKHIN. Excuse me, Charlotta Ivanovna, I haven't had time yet to welcome you back. (*Tries to kiss her hand.*)

CHARLOTTA (*pulling her hand away*). If I let you kiss a hand, next you'd be after a elbow, then a shoulder . . .

LOPAKHIN. My unlucky day.

Everybody laughs.

Charlotta Ivanovna, show us a trick!

LYUBOV ANDREEVNA. Charlotta, show us a trick!

CHARLOTTA. Nothing doing. I want to go to bed. (*Exits.*)

LOPAKHIN. Three weeks from now we'll meet again. (*Kisses Lyubov Andreevna's hand.*) Meanwhile, good-bye. It's time. (*To Gaev.*) Be suing you.[29] (*Exchanges kisses with Pishchik.*) Be suing you. (*Gives his hand to Varya, then to Firs and Yasha.*) I don't want to go. (*To Lyubov Andreevna.*) If you reconsider this cottage business and come to a decision, then let me know, I'll arrange a loan of fifty thousand or so. Give it some serious thought.

VARYA (*angrily*). Well, go if you're going!

LOPAKHIN. I'm going, I'm going . . . (*He leaves.*)

GAEV. Oaf. All right, *pardon* . . . Varya's going to marry him, that's our Varya's little intended!

---

29 Instead of *Do svidaniya*, "Be seeing you," Lopakhin facetiously says *Do svidantsiya*.

VARYA. Don't say anything uncalled for, uncle dear.

LYUBOV ANDREEVNA. So what, Varya, I'll be very glad. He's a good man.

PISHCHIK. A man, you've got to tell the truth . . . most worthy . . . And my Dashenka . . . also says that . . . says all sorts of things. (*Snores but immediately wakes up.*) But by the way, most respected lady, lend me . . . . two hundred and forty rubles . . . tomorrow I've got to pay the interest on the mortgage . . .[30]

VARYA (*alarmed*). We're all out, all out!

LYUBOV ANDREEVNA. As a matter of fact, I haven't a thing.

PISHCHIK. It'll turn up. (*Laughs.*) I never lose hope. There, I think, all is lost, I'm a goner, lo and behold! — the railroad runs across my land and . . . pays me for it. And then, watch, something else will happen sooner or later . . . Dashenka will win two hundred thousand . . . she's got a lottery ticket.

LYUBOV ANDREEVNA. The coffee's finished, now we can go to bed.

FIRS (*brushes Gaev's clothes, scolding*). You didn't put on them trousers again. What am I going to do with you!

---

30 By 1903, almost one-half of all private land in Russia (excluding peasant land) was mortgaged, forcing the landed gentry to sell their estates and join the professional or commercial classes, as Gaev does at the end of this play.

VARYA (*quietly*). Anya's asleep. (*Quietly opens a window.*) The sun's up already, it's not so cold. Look, Mama dear, what wonderful trees! My goodness, the air! The starlings are singing!

GAEV (*opens another window*). The orchard's all white. You haven't forgotten, Lyuba? There's that long pathway leading straight on, straight on, like a stretched ribbon, it glistens on moonlit nights. You remember? You haven't forgotten?

LYUBOV ANDREEVNA (*looks through the window at the orchard*). O, my childhood, my innocence! I slept in this nursery, gazed out at the orchard, happiness awoke with me every morning, and it was just the same then, nothing has changed. (*Laughs with joy.*) All, all white! O, my orchard! After the dark, drizzly autumn and the cold winter, you're young again, full of happiness, the angels in heaven haven't forsaken you . . . If only I could lift off my chest and shoulders this heavy stone, if only I could forget my past!

GAEV. Yes, and the orchard will be sold for debts, strange as it seems . . .

LYUBOV ANDREEVNA. Look, our poor Mama is walking through the orchard . . . in a white dress! (*Laughs with joy.*) There she is.

GAEV. Where?

VARYA. God keep you, Mama dear.

LYUBOV ANDREEVNA. There's nobody there, it just seemed so to me. On the right, by the turning to the summerhouse, a white sapling was bending, it looked like a woman . . .

Enter TROFIMOV, in a shabby student's uniform and eyeglasses.[31]

What a marvelous orchard! White bunches of blossoms, blue sky . . .

TROFIMOV. Lyubov Andreevna! (*She has stared round at him.*) I'll just pay my respects and then leave at once. (*Kisses her hand fervently.*) They told me to wait till morning, but I didn't have the patience . . .

LYUBOV ANDREEVNA stares in bewilderment.

VARYA (*through tears*). This is Petya Trofimov.

TROFIMOV. Petya Trofimov, used to be tutor to your Grisha . . . Can I have changed so much?

LYUBOV ANDREEVNA embraces him and weeps quietly.

GAEV (*embarrassed*). Come, come, Lyuba.

VARYA (*weeps*). Didn't I tell you, Petya, to wait till tomorrow.

LYUBOV ANDREEVNA. My Grisha . . . my little boy . . . Grisha . . . my son . . .

---

31 "I'm worried about the second act's lack of action and a certain sketchy quality in Trofimov, the student. After all, time and again Trofimov is being sent into exile, time and again he is being expelled from the university, but how can you express stuff like that?" (Chekhov to Olga Knipper, October 19, 1903).

VARYA. There's no help for it, Mama dear, God's will be done.

TROFIMOV (*gently, through tears*). There, there . . .

LYUBOV ANDREEVNA (*quietly weeping*). A little boy lost, drowned . . . What for? What for, my friend? (*More quietly.*) Anya's asleep in there, and I'm so loud . . . making noise . . . Well now, Petya? Why have you become so homely? Why have you got old?

TROFIMOV. On the train, a peasant woman called me: that scruffy gent.

LYUBOV ANDREEVNA. You were just a boy in those days, a dear little student, but now your hair is thinning, eyeglasses. Are you really still a student? (*Goes to the door.*)

TROFIMOV. I suppose I'll be a perpetual student.[32]

LYUBOV ANDREEVNA (*kisses her brother, then Varya*). Well, let's go to bed . . . You've got old too, Leonid.

PISHCHIK (*follows her*). That means it's time for bed . . . Ugh, my gout. I'll stay over with you . . . And if you would, Lyubov Andreevna, dear heart, tomorrow morning early . . . two hundred and forty rubles . . .

GAEV. He never gives up.

---

32 Radical student dropouts were far from uncommon. The saying went, "It takes ten years to graduate—five in study, four in exile, and one wasted while the University is shut down."

PISHCHIK. Two hundred and forty rubles . . . to pay the interest on the mortgage.

LYUBOV ANDREEVNA. I have no money, darling . . .

PISHCHIK. We'll pay it back, dear lady . . . The most trifling sum.

LYUBOV ANDREEVNA. Well, all right, Leonid will let you have it . . . Let him have it, Leonid.

GAEV. I'll let him have it, hold out your pockets.

LYUBOV ANDREEVNA. What can we do, let him have it . . . He needs it . . . He'll pay it back.

> LYUBOV ANDREEVNA, TROFIMOV,
> PISHCHIK, and FIRS go out. GAEV, VARYA, and
> YASHA remain.

GAEV. My sister still hasn't outgrown the habit of squandering money. (*To Yasha.*) Out of the way, my good man, you smell like a chicken coop.

YASHA (*with a sneer*). But you, Leonid Andreich, are just the same as you were.

GAEV. How's that? (*To Varya.*) What did he say?

VARYA (*to Yasha*). Your mother's come from the village, since yesterday she's been sitting in the servants' hall, she wants to see you . . .

YASHA. To hell with her!

VARYA. Ah, disgraceful!

YASHA. That's all I need. She could have come tomorrow. (*Exits.*)

VARYA. Mama dear is just as she was before, she hasn't changed a bit. If it were up to her, she'd give away everything.

GAEV. Yes . . .

Pause.

If a large number of cures is suggested for a particular disease, it means the disease is incurable. I think, wrack my brains, I've come up with all sorts of solutions, all sorts, which means, actually, none. It would be nice to inherit a fortune from somebody, nice if we married our Anya to a very rich man, nice to go to Yaroslavl and try our luck with our auntie the Countess. Auntie's really very, very wealthy.

VARYA (*weeps*). If only God would come to our aid.

GAEV. Stop sniveling. Auntie's very wealthy, but she isn't fond of us. In the first place, Sister married a lawyer, not a nobleman . . .

ANYA appears in the doorway.

Married a commoner and behaved herself, well, you can't say very virtuously. She's a good, kind, splendid person, I love her very much, but, no matter how you consider the extenuating circumstances, you still have to admit she's depraved. You can feel it in her slightest movement.

VARYA (*whispering*). Anya's standing in the doorway.

GAEV. How's that?

Pause.

Extraordinary, something's got in my right eye . . . my sight's beginning to fail. And Thursday, when I was at the county courthouse . . .

ANYA enters.

VARYA. Why aren't you asleep, Anya?

ANYA. I can't fall asleep. I can't.

GAEV. My teeny-weeny. (*Kisses Anya's face, hands.*) My little girl . . . (*Through tears.*) You're not my niece, you're my angel, you're everything to me. Believe me, believe . . .

ANYA. I believe you, Uncle. Everybody loves you, respects you . . . but dear Uncle, you must keep still, simply keep still. What were you saying just now about my Mama, your own sister? How come you said that?

GAEV. Yes, yes . . . (*Hides his face in his hands.*) It's an awful thing to say! My God! God help me! And today I made a speech to the cupboard . . . like a fool! And as soon as I'd finished, I realized what a fool I'd been.

VARYA. True, Uncle dear, you ought to keep still. Just keep still, that's all.

ANYA. If you keep still, you'll be more at peace with yourself.

GAEV. I'll keep still. (*Kisses Anya's and Varya's hands.*) I'll keep still. Only this is business. Thursday I was at the county courthouse, well, some friends gathered round, started talking about this and that, six of one, half a dozen of the other, and it turns out a person can sign a promissory note and borrow money to pay the interest to the bank.

VARYA. If only God would come to our aid!

GAEV. I'll go there on Tuesday and have another talk. (*To Varya.*) Stop sniveling. (*To Anya.*) Your Mama will talk to Lopakhin, he won't refuse her, of course . . . And you, after you've had a rest, will go to Yaroslavl to the Countess, your great-aunt. That way we'll have action on three fronts—and our business is in the bag! We'll pay off the interest, I'm sure of it . . . (*Pops a candy into his mouth.*) Word of honor, I'll swear by whatever you like, the estate won't be sold! (*Excited.*) I swear by my happiness! Here's my hand on it, call me a trashy, dishonorable man if I permit that auction! I swear with every fiber of my being!

ANYA (*a more peaceful mood comes over her, she is happy*). You're so good, Uncle, so clever! (*Embraces her uncle.*) Now I feel calm! I'm calm! I'm happy!

Enter FIRS.

FIRS (*scolding*). Leonid Andreich, have you no fear of God? When are you going to bed?

GAEV. Right away, right away. Go along, Firs. Have it your own way, I'll undress myself. Well, children, beddie-bye . . . Details tomorrow, but for now go to bed. (*Kisses Anya and Varya.*) I'm a man of the eighties . . . People don't put much stock in that period,[33] but all the same I can say I've suffered for my convictions to no small degree in my time. There's a good reason peasants love me. You've got to study peasants! You've got to know what . . .

ANYA. You're at it again, Uncle!

VARYA. Uncle dear, you must keep still.

FIRS (*angrily*). Leonid Andreich!

GAEV. Coming, coming . . . You two go to bed. Two cushion carom to the center! I sink the white . . . (*Exits followed by Firs, hobbling.*)

ANYA. Now I'm calm. I don't want to go to Yaroslavl. I don't like my great-aunt, but all the same, I'm calm. Thanks to Uncle. (*Sits down.*)

VARYA. Got to get some sleep. I'm off. Oh, while you were away there was a bit of an uprising. There's nobody living in the old servants' hall, as you know, except the old servants: Yefimushka, Polya, Yevstigney, oh, and Karp. They started letting these vagabonds spend the night there—I held my peace. Only then, I hear, they've spread the rumor that I gave orders to feed them nothing but beans. Out of stinginess, you see . . . And this was

---

33 Under Alexander III, political reaction to reforms set in, the police and censorship became extremely repressive, and anti-Semitic pogroms broke out. Large-scale political reform became impossible, so that liberal intellectuals devoted themselves to local civilizing improvements in the villages, Tolstoyan passive resistance, and dabbling in "art for art's sake." This feeling of social and political impotence led to the torpid aimlessness common to Chekhov's characters.

all Yevstigney's doing . . . Fine, I think. If that's how things are, I think, just you wait. I send for Yevstigney . . . (*Yawns.*) In he comes . . . What's wrong with you, I say, Yevstigney . . . you're such an idiot . . . (*Glancing at Anya.*) Anechka!

Pause.

Fast asleep! . . . (*Takes Anya by the arm.*) Let's go to bed . . . Let's go! . . . (*Leads her.*) My darling is fast asleep! Let's go! . . .

They go out.

Far beyond the orchard, a shepherd is playing his pipes.

TROFIMOV crosses the stage and, seeing Anya and Varya, stops short.

Ssh . . . She's asleep . . . asleep . . . Let's go, dearest.

ANYA (*softly, half-asleep*). I'm so tired . . . all the sleigh bells . . . Uncle . . . dear . . . and Mama and Uncle . . .

VARYA. Let's go, dearest, let's go . . . (*They go into Anya's room.*)

TROFIMOV (*moved*). My sunshine! My springtime!

Curtain

ACT TWO

*A field. An old, long-abandoned shrine leaning to
one side, beside it a well, large slabs that were once,
apparently, tombstones, and an old bench. A road
into Gaev's estate can be seen. At one side, towering
poplars cast their shadows; here the cherry orchard
begins. Farther off are telegraph poles, and way in
the distance, dimly sketched on the horizon, is a
large town, which can be seen only in the best and
clearest weather. Soon the sun will set. CHARLOTTA,
YASHA, and DUNYASHA are sitting on the bench.
YEPIKHODOV stands nearby and strums a guitar;
everyone is rapt in thought. CHARLOTTA is wearing
an old peaked cap with a vizor; she has taken a rifle
off her shoulder and is adjusting a buckle on the strap.*

CHARLOTTA (*pensively*). I haven't got a valid passport,[34] I don't
know how old I am, and I always feel like I'm still oh so young.
When I was a little girl, my father and momma used to go from
fairground to fairground, giving performances, pretty good

---

34 In the sense of an "internal passport," an identity document carried when traveling
through the Russian empire.

ones. And I would do the death-defying leap[35] and all sorts of stunts. And when Poppa and Momma died, a German gentle-woman took me home with her and started teaching me. Fine. I grew up, then turned into a governess. But where I'm from and who I am—I don't know . . . Who my parents were, maybe they weren't married . . . I don't know. (*Pulls a pickle out of her pocket and eats it.*) I don't know anything.

Pause.

It would be nice to talk to someone, but there is no one . . . I have no one.

YEPIKHODOV (*strums his guitar and sings*). "What care I for the noisy world, what are friends and foes to me . . ." How pleasant to play the mandolin!

DUNYASHA. That's a guitar, not a mandolin. (*Looks in a hand mirror and powders her nose.*)

YEPIKHODOV. To a lovesick lunatic, this is a mandolin . . . (*Sings quietly.*) "Were but my heart aflame with the spark of requited love . . ."

YASHA joins in.

CHARLOTTA. Horrible the way these people sing . . . Phooey! A pack of hyenas.

---

35 In the original, Italian, *salto mortale.*

DUNYASHA (*to Yasha*). Anyway, how lucky to spend time abroad.

YASHA. Yes, of course. I can't disagree with you there. (*Yawns, then lights a cigar.*)

YEPIKHODOV. Stands to reason. Abroad everything long ago attained its complete complexification.

YASHA. Goes without saying.

YEPIKHODOV. I'm a cultured person, I read all kinds of remarkable books, but somehow I can't figure out my inclinations, what I want personally, to live or to shoot myself, speaking on my own behalf, nevertheless I always carry a revolver on my person. Here it is . . . (*Displays a revolver.*)

CHARLOTTA. I'm done. Now I'll go. (*Shoulders the gun.*) Yepikhodov, you're a very clever fellow, and a very frightening one; the women ought to love you madly. Brrr! (*On her way out.*) These clever people are all so stupid there's no one for me to talk to . . . No one . . . All alone, alone, I've got no one and . . . who I am, why I am, I don't know. (*Exits.*)

YEPIKHODOV. Speaking on my own behalf, not flying off on tangents, I must express myself about myself, among others, that Fate treats me ruthlessly, like a small storm-tossed ship. If, suppose, I'm wrong about this, then why when I woke up this morning, to give but a single example, I look and there on my chest is a ghastly enormity of a spider . . . Like so. (*Uses both hands to demonstrate.*) Or then again, I'll take some kvas, so as

to drink it, and lo and behold, there'll be something indecent
to the nth degree, along the lines of a cockroach . . .

Pause.

Have you read Buckle?[36]

Pause.

I should like to distress you, Avdotya Fyodorovna, with a couple
of words.

DUNYASHA. Go ahead.

YEPIKHODOV. I would be desirous to see you in private . . . (*Sighs.*)

DUNYASHA (*embarrassed*). All right . . . only fiıst bring me my
wrap . . .[37] It's next to the cupboard . . . it's a bit damp here.

YEPIKHODOV. Yes, ma'am . . . I'll fetch it, ma'am . . . . Now I
know what I have to do with my revolver . . . (*Takes the guitar
and exits playing it.*)

YASHA. Tons of Trouble! Pretty stupid, take it from me. (*Yawns.*)

---

36 Henry Thomas Buckle (1821–1862), pronounced Buckly, whose *History of Civilization in England* (translated into Russian in 1861) posited that skepticism was the
handmaiden of progress and that religion retards the advance of civilization. His
materialist approach was much appreciated by progressive Russians in the 1870s, and
Chekhov had read him as a student. By the end of the century Buckle's ideas seemed
outmoded, so the reference suggests that Yepikhodov's efforts at self-education are
behind the times.

37 *Talmochka*, or little talma, a smaller version of a quilted, full-length cloak, named
after Napoleon's favorite tragic actor.

DUNYASHA. God forbid he should shoot himself.

Pause.

I've got jittery, nervous all the time. Just a little girl, they brought me to the master's house, now I'm out of touch with ordinary life, and my hands are white as white can be, like a young lady's. I've got sensitive, so delicate, ladylike, afraid of every little thing . . . Awfully so. And, Yasha, if you deceive me, then I don't know what'll happen to my nerves.

YASHA (*kisses her*). Tasty little pickle! Of course, a girl ought to know how far to go, and if there's one thing I hate, it's a girl who misbehaves . . .

DUNYASHA. I love you ever so much, you're educated, you can discuss anything.

Pause.

YASHA (*yawns*). Yes'm . . . The way I look at it, it's like this: if a girl loves somebody, that means she's immoral.

Pause.

Nice smoking a cigar in the fresh air . . . (*Listening.*) Someone's coming this way . . . The masters . . .

DUNYASHA impulsively embraces him.

Go home, pretend you'd been to the river for a swim, take this bypath or you'll run into them, and they'll think I've been going out with you. I couldn't stand that.

DUNYASHA (*coughs quietly*). Your cigar's given me a headache . . . (*Exits.*)

*YASHA remains, seated beside the shrine. Enter
LYUBOV ANDREEVNA, GAEV, and LOPAKHIN.*

LOPAKHIN. You've got to decide once and for all—time won't stand still. The matter's really simple, after all. Do you agree to rent land for cottages or not? Give me a one-word answer: yes or no? Just one word!

LYUBOV ANDREEVNA. Who's been smoking those revolting cigars around here . . . (*Sits.*)

GAEV. Now that there's a railroad, things are convenient.[38] (*Sits.*) You ride to town and have lunch . . . yellow to the center! I should go home first, play one game . . .

LYUBOV ANDREEVNA. You'll have time.

LOPAKHIN. Just one word! (*Pleading.*) Give me an answer!

GAEV (*yawning*). How's that?

LYUBOV ANDREEVNA (*looking into her purse*). Yesterday I had lots of money, but today there's very little left. My poor Varya feeds everybody milk soup to economize, in the kitchen the old people get nothing but beans, and somehow I'm spending

---

38 There was a railway boom in Russia in the 1890s, although, owing to bribery and corruption, the stations were often some distance from the towns, and the service was far from efficient.

recklessly . . . (*Drops the purse, scattering gold coins.*) Oh dear, they've spilled all over . . . (*Annoyed.*)

YASHA. Allow me, I'll pick them up at once. (*Gathers the money.*)

LYUBOV ANDREEVNA. That's sweet of you, Yasha. And why did I go out to lunch . . . That nasty restaurant of yours with its music, the tablecloths smelt of soap . . . Why drink so much, Lyonya? Why eat so much? Why talk so much? Today in the restaurant you started talking a lot again and all beside the point. About the seventies, about the decadents.[39] And who to? Talking to waiters about the decadents!

LOPAKHIN. Yes.

GAEV (*waves his hand in dismissal*). I'm incorrigible, it's obvious . . . (*Irritably, to Yasha.*) What's the matter, forever whirling around in front of us . . .

YASHA (*laughing*). I can't hear your voice without laughing.

GAEV (*to his sister*). Either he goes or I do . . .

LYUBOV ANDREEVNA. Go away, Yasha, run along . . .

YASHA (*handing the purse to Lyubov Andreevna*). I'll go right now. (*Barely keeping from laughing.*) Right this minute . . .

---

39 A period when the intelligentsia formed the *Narodniki*, or Populists, who preached a socialist doctrine and tried to educate the peasants. They were severely repressed in 1877–1878. Decadents here refers to writers of symbolist literature.

Exits.

LOPAKHIN. Deriganov the rich man intends to purchase your estate. They says he's coming to the auction in person.

LYUBOV ANDREEVNA. Where did you hear that?

LOPAKHIN. They were talking about it in town.

GAEV. Our auntie in Yaroslavl promised to send something, but when or how much she'll send, we don't know . . .

LOPAKHIN. How much is she sending? A hundred thousand? Two hundred?

LYUBOV ANDREEVNA. Well . . . around ten or fifteen thousand, and we're glad to have it . . .

LOPAKHIN. Excuse me, such frivolous people as you, my friends, such unbusinesslike, peculiar people I've never run into before. Somebody tells you in plain words your estate is about to be sold, and you act as if you don't understand.

LYUBOV ANDREEVNA. But what are we supposed to do? Teach us, what?

LOPAKHIN. I teach you every day. Every day I tell you one and the same thing. Both the cherry orchard and the land have got to be leased as lots for cottages, do it right now, immediately— the auction is staring you in the face! Can't you understand! Decide once and for all that there'll be cottages, they'll lend you as much money as you want, and then you'll be saved.

LYUBOV ANDREEVNA. Cottages and vacationers—it's so vulgar, excuse me.

GAEV. I absolutely agree with you.

LOPAKHIN. I'll burst into tears or scream or fall down in a faint. It's too much for me! You're torturing me to death! (*To Gaev.*) You old biddy!

GAEV. How's that?

LOPAKHIN. Old biddy! (*Starts to exit.*)

LYUBOV ANDREEVNA (*frightened*). No, don't go, stay, dovey . . . Please. Maybe we'll think of something.

LOPAKHIN. What's there to think about?

LYUBOV ANDREEVNA. Don't go, please. With you here somehow it's more fun . . .

Pause.

I keep anticipating something, as if the house were about to collapse on top of us.

GAEV (*rapt in thought*). Off the cushion to the corner . . . doublette to the center . . .

LYUBOV ANDREEVNA. We've sinned so very much . . .

LOPAKHIN. What kind of sins have you got . . .

GAEV (*pops a hard candy into his mouth*). They say I've eaten up my whole estate in hard candies . . . (*Laughs.*)

LYUBOV ANDREEVNA. Oh, my sins . . . I've always thrown money around wildly, like a maniac, and married a man who produced nothing but debts. My husband died of champagne—he was a terrible drunkard,—and, then, to add to my troubles, I fell in love with another man, had an affair, and just at that time—this was my first punishment, dropped right on my head,—over there in the river . . . my little boy drowned, and I went abroad, went for good, never to return, never to see that river again . . . I shut my eyes, ran away, out of my mind, and *he* came after me . . . cruelly, brutally. I bought a villa near Mentone, because he fell ill there, and for three years I didn't know what it was to rest day or night: the invalid wore me out, my heart shriveled up. But last year, when the villa was sold to pay my debts, I went to Paris, and there he robbed me, ran off, had an affair with another woman, I tried to poison myself . . . so silly, so shameful . . . and suddenly I was drawn back to Russia, to my country, to my little girl . . . (*Wipes away her tears.*) Lord, Lord, be merciful, forgive me my sins! Don't punish me anymore! (*Takes a telegram out of her pocket.*) I received this today from Paris . . . He begs my forgiveness, implores me to come back . . . (*Tears up telegram.*) Sounds like music somewhere. (*Listens.*)

GAEV. That's our famous Jewish orchestra. You remember, four fiddles, a flute, and a double bass.

LYUBOV ANDREEVNA. Does it still exist? We ought to hire them sometime and throw a party.

LOPAKHIN (*listening*). I don't hear it . . . (*Sings softly.*) "And for cash the Prussians will frenchify the Russians." (*Laughs.*) That was some play I saw at the theater yesterday, very funny.

LYUBOV ANDREEVNA. And most likely there was nothing funny about it. You have no business looking at plays, you should look at yourselves more. You all live such gray lives, you talk such nonsense.

LOPAKHIN. That's true, I've got to admit, this life of ours is idiotic . . .

Pause.

My dad was a peasant, an imbecile, he didn't understand anything, didn't teach me, all he did was get drunk and beat me, with the same old stick. Deep down, I'm the same kind of blockhead and imbecile. I never studied anything, my handwriting is disgusting, I write, I'm ashamed to show it to people, like a pig.

LYUBOV ANDREEVNA. You ought to get married, my friend.

LOPAKHIN. Yes . . . that's true.

LYUBOV ANDREEVNA. You should marry our Varya; she's a good girl.

LOPAKHIN. Yes.

LYUBOV ANDREEVNA. She came to me from peasant stock, she works all day long, but the main thing is she loves you. Besides, you've been fond of her a long time.

LOPAKHIN. Why not? I'm not against it . . . She's a good girl.

Pause.

GAEV. They're offering me a position at the bank. Six thousand a year . . . Have you heard?

LYUBOV ANDREEVNA. You indeed! Stay where you are . . .

FIRS enters, carrying an overcoat.

FIRS (*to Gaev*). Please, sir, put it on, or you'll get wet.

GAEV (*putting on the overcoat*). You're a pest, my man.

FIRS. Never you mind . . . This morning you went out, didn't tell nobody. (*Inspects him.*)

LYUBOV ANDREEVNA. How old you're getting, Firs!

FIRS. What's wanted?

LOPAKHIN. The mistress says, you're getting very old!

FIRS. I've lived a long time. They were making plans to marry me off, long before your daddy even saw the light . . . (*Laughs.*) And when freedom came,[40] I was already head footman. I didn't go along with freedom then, I stayed by the masters . . .

---

40 Alexander II emancipated the serfs in 1861.

Pause.

And I recollect they was all glad, but what they was glad about, that they didn't know.

LOPAKHIN. It used to be nice all right. In those days you could at least get flogged.

FIRS (*not having heard*). I'll say. The peasants stood by the masters, the masters stood by the peasants, but now things is every which way, you can't figure it out.

GAEV. Keep quiet, Firs. Tomorrow I have to go to town. They promised to introduce me to some general, who might make us a loan on an I.O.U.

LOPAKHIN. Nothing'll come of it. And you won't pay the interest, never fear.

LYUBOV ANDREEVNA. He's raving. There are no such generals.

Enter TROFIMOV, ANYA, and VARYA.

GAEV. Look, here comes our crowd.

ANYA. Mama's sitting down.

LYUBOV ANDREEVNA (*tenderly*). Come here, come . . . My darlings . . . (*Embracing Anya and Varya.*) If only you both knew how much I love you. Sit beside me, that's right.

Everyone sits down.

LOPAKHIN. Our perpetual student is always stepping out with the young ladies.

TROFIMOV. None of your business.

LOPAKHIN. Soon he'll be fifty and he'll still be a student.

TROFIMOV. Stop your idiotic jokes.

LOPAKHIN. What are you getting angry about, you crank?

TROFIMOV. Stop pestering me.

LOPAKHIN (*laughs*). And may I ask, what do you make of me?

TROFIMOV. This is what I make of you, Yermolay Alekseich: you're a rich man, soon you'll be a millionaire. And just as an essential component in the conversion of matter is the wild beast that devours whatever crosses its path, you're essential.

Everyone laughs.

VARYA. Petya, tell us about the planets instead.

LYUBOV ANDREEVNA. No, let's go on with yesterday's discussion.

TROFIMOV. What was that about?

GAEV. Human pride.[41]

TROFIMOV. Yesterday we talked for quite a while, but we didn't get anywhere. Human pride, as you see it, has something mys-

---

41 A reference to Maksim Gorky's "Proud man" in the play *The Lower Depths* (1902). "Hu-man Be-ing! That's magnificent! That sounds . . . proud!" "Man is truth . . . He is the be-all and the end-all. Nothing exists but man, all the rest is the work of his hands and his brain. Man is something great, proud, man is."

tical about it. Maybe you're right from your point of view, but if we reason it out simply, without frills, what's the point of human pride, what's the sense of it, if man is poorly constructed physiologically, if the vast majority is crude, unthinking, profoundly wretched. We should stop admiring ourselves. We should just work.

GAEV. All the same you'll die.

TROFIMOV. Who knows? What does that mean—you'll die? Maybe man has a hundred senses and in death only the five we know perish, the remaining ninety-five live on.

LYUBOV ANDREEVNA. Aren't you clever, Petya! . . .

LOPAKHIN (*ironically*). Awfully!

TROFIMOV. Mankind is advancing, perfecting its powers. Everything that's unattainable for us now will some day come within our grasp and our understanding, only we've got to work, to help the truth seekers with all our might. So far here in Russia, very few people do any work. The vast majority of educated people, as I know them, pursues nothing, does nothing, and so far isn't capable of work. They call themselves intellectuals, but they refer to the servants by pet names,[42] treat the peasants like animals, are poorly informed, read nothing serious, do absolutely nothing, just talk about science, barely understand art.

---

42 Literally, "they address the servant girl with the familiar form of 'you,' " as Lopakhin does Dunyasha. It is typical of Trofimov's intellectual astigmatism that he demands token respect for the servant class but cannot foresee doing away with it entirely.

They're all earnest, they all have serious faces, they all talk only about major issues, they philosophize, but meanwhile anybody can see that the working class is abominably fed, sleeps without pillows, thirty or forty to a room, everywhere bedbugs, stench,[43] damp, moral pollution . . . So obviously all our nice chitchat serves only to shut our eyes to ourselves and to others. Show me, where are the day-care centers we talk so much about, where are the reading rooms? People only write about them in novels, in fact there aren't any. There's only dirt, vulgarity, Asiatic inertia . . .[44] I'm afraid of, I don't like very earnest faces, I'm afraid of earnest discussions. It's better to keep still!

LOPAKHIN. You know, I get up before five every morning. I work from dawn to dusk, well, I always have money on hand, my own and other people's, and I can tell what the people around me are like. You only have to go into business to find out how few decent, honest people there are. Sometimes, when I can't sleep, I think: Lord, you gave us vast forests, boundless fields, the widest horizons, and living here, we really and truly ought to be giants . . .

LYUBOV ANDREEVNA. So you want to have giants . . . They're only good in fairy tales, anywhere else they're scary.

---

43 The line beginning "Anyone can see" and ending "moral pollution" was deleted by Chekhov to accommodate the censor, and restored only in 1917. It was replaced by a line reading, "the vast majority of us, ninety-nine percent, live like savages, at the least provocation swearing and punching one another in the mouth, eating nauseating food, sleeping in mud and foul air."

44 *Aziatchina*, a pre-Revolutionary term of abuse, referring to negative qualities in the Russian character such as laziness and inefficiency.

Far upstage YEPIKHODOV crosses and plays his
guitar.

LYUBOV ANDREEVNA (*dreamily*). There goes Yepikhodov . . .

ANYA (*dreamily*). There goes Yepikhodov . . .

GAEV. The sun has set, ladies and gentlemen.

TROFIMOV. Yes.

GAEV (*quietly, as if declaiming*). Oh Nature, wondrous creature, aglow with eternal radiance, beautiful yet impassive, you whom we call Mother, merging within yourself Life and Death, you nourish and you destroy . . .

VARYA (*pleading*). Uncle dear!

ANYA. Uncle, you're at it again!

TROFIMOV. You'd better bank the yellow in the center dou-blette.

GAEV. I'll be still, I'll be still.

> *Everyone sits, absorbed in thought. The only sound*
> *is FIRS, softly muttering. Suddenly a distant sound*
> *is heard, as if from the sky, the sound of a breaking*
> *string, dying away, mournfully.* [45]

---

45 According to the literary critic Batyushkov, Chekhov put great stock in this sound. The author told him that Stanislavsky, not yet having read the play, asked him about the sound effects it ought to have. "'In one of the acts I have an offstage sound, a complicated kind of sound which cannot be described in a few words, but it is very

LYUBOV ANDREEVNA. What's that?

LOPAKHIN. I don't know. Somewhere far off in a mineshaft the rope broke on a bucket.[46] But somewhere very far off.

GAEV. Or perhaps it was some kind of bird . . . something like a heron.

TROFIMOV. Or an owl . . .

LYUBOV ANDREEVNA (*shivers*). Unpleasant anyhow.

Pause.

FIRS. Before the troubles, it was the same: the screech owl hooted and the samovar never stopped humming.

GAEV. Before what troubles?

FIRS. Before freedom.[47]

Pause.

LYUBOV ANDREEVNA. You know, everyone, we should go home. Evening's drawing on. (*To Anya.*) You've got tears in your eyes . . . What is it, little girl? (*Kisses her.*)

---

important that this sound be exactly the way I want it.' . . . 'Is the sound really that important?' I asked. Anton Pavlovich looked at me sternly and said, 'It is.' "

46 This was a sound Chekhov remembered hearing as a boy. In his story "Happiness," he uses it ironically as a spectral laugh, presaging disappointment.

47 Under the terms of the Emancipation Act, field peasants were allotted land but had to pay back the government in annual installments the sum used to indemnify former landowners. House serfs, on the other hand, were allotted no land. Both these conditions caused tremendous hardship and were responsible for great unrest among the newly manumitted.

ANYA. Nothing special, Mama. Never mind.

TROFIMOV. Someone's coming.

> A VAGRANT appears in a shabby white peaked cap
> and an overcoat; he is tipsy.

VAGRANT. May I inquire, can I get directly to the station from here?

GAEV. You can. Follow that road.

VAGRANT. Obliged to you from the bottom of my heart. (*Coughs.*) Splendid weather we're having . . . (*Declaims.*) "Brother mine, suffering brother . . . come to the Volga, whose laments . . ."[48] (*To Varya.*) Mademoiselle, bestow a mere thirty kopeks on a famished fellow Russian . . .

> VARYA is alarmed, screams.

LOPAKHIN (*angrily*). A person's allowed to be rude only so far![49]

LYUBOV ANDREEVNA (*flustered*). Take this . . . here you are . . . (*Looks in her purse.*) No silver . . . Never mind, here's a gold piece for you . . .

VAGRANT. Obliged to you from the bottom of my heart! (*Exits.*)

---

48 The Vagrant quotes from a popular and populist poem of 1881 by Semyon Yakovlevich Nadson (1862–1887) and from Nekrasov's "Reflections at the Main Gate" (1858). The laments are supposed to come from barge haulers along the Volga. Quoting Nekrasov is always a sign of insincerity in Chekhov.

49 In Russian, Lopakin's remark is very awkwardly phrased.

Laughter.

VARYA (*frightened*). I'm going . . . I'm going . . . Oh, Mama dear, there's nothing in the house for people to eat, and you gave him a gold piece.

LYUBOV ANDREEVNA. What can you do with a silly like me? I'll let you have all I've got when we get home. Yermolay Alekse-ich, lend me some more! . . .

LOPAKHIN. At your service.

LYUBOV ANDREEVNA. Come along, ladies and gentlemen, it's time. And look, Varya, we've made quite a match for you, congratulations.

VARYA (*through tears*). It's no joking matter, Mama.

LOPAKHIN. I'll feel ya,[50] get thee to a nunnery . . .

GAEV. My hands are trembling; it's been a long time since I played billiards.

LOPAKHIN. I'll feel ya, o nymph, in thy horizons be all my sins remembered![51]

LYUBOV ANDREEVNA. Come along, ladies and gentlemen. Almost time for supper.

---

50 *Okhmeliya*, from *okhmelyat*, to get drunk, instead of Ophelia.

51 Lopakhin is misquoting Hamlet, "Nymph, in thy orisons, be all my sins remember'd" (Act III, scene 1).

VARYA. He scared me. My heart's pounding.

LOPAKHIN. I remind you, ladies and gentlemen, on the twenty-second of August the estate will be auctioned off. Think about that! . . . Think! . . .

Everyone leaves except TROFIMOV and ANYA.

ANYA (*laughing*). Thank the vagrant, he scared off Varya, now we're alone.

TROFIMOV. Varya's afraid we'll suddenly fall in love, so she hangs around us all day. Her narrow mind can't comprehend that we're above love. Avoiding the petty and specious that keeps us from being free and happy, that's the goal and meaning of our life. Forward! We march irresistibly toward the shining star, glowing there in the distance! Forward! No dropping behind, friends!

ANYA (*stretching up her arms*). You speak so well!

Pause.

It's wonderful here today.

TROFIMOV. Yes, superb weather.

ANYA. What have you done to me, Petya, why have I stopped loving the cherry orchard as I used to? I loved it so tenderly, there seemed to me no finer place on earth than our orchard.

TROFIMOV. All Russia is our orchard. The world is wide and beautiful and there are many wonderful places in it.

Pause.

Just think, Anya: your grandfather, great-grandfather, and all your ancestors were slave owners, they owned living souls, and from every cherry in the orchard, every leaf, every tree trunk there must be human beings watching you, you must hear voices . . . They owned living souls—it's corrupted all of you, honestly, those who lived before and those living now, so that your mother, you, your uncle, no longer notice that you're living in debt, at other people's expense, at the expense of those people whom you wouldn't even let beyond your front hall . . .[52] We're at least two hundred years behind the times, we've still got absolutely nothing, no definite attitude to the past, we just philosophize, complain of depression, or drink vodka. It's so clear, isn't it, that before we start living in the present, we must first atone for our past, put an end to it, and we can atone for it only through suffering, only through extraordinary, unremitting labor. Understand that, Anya.

ANYA. The house we live in hasn't been our house for a long time, and I'll go away, I give you my word.

TROFIMOV. If you have the housekeeper's keys, throw them down the well and go away. Be free as the wind.

---

52 The line beginning "They owned living souls" and ending "your front hall" was deleted by Chekhov to accommodate the censor and restored only in 1917. It was replaced with this line: "Oh, it's dreadful, your orchard is terrifying. At evening or at night when you walk through the orchard, the old bark on the trees begins to glow and it seems as if the cherry trees are dreaming of what went on one or two hundred years ago, and painful nightmares make them droop. Why talk about it?"

ANYA (*enraptured*). You speak so well!

TROFIMOV. Believe me, Anya, believe! I'm not yet thirty, I'm young. I'm still a student, but I've already undergone so much! When winter comes, I'm starved, sick, anxious, poor as a beggar and—where haven't I been chased by Fate, where haven't I been! And yet always, every moment of the day and night, my soul has been full of inexplicable foreboding. I foresee happiness, Anya, I can see it already . . .

ANYA (*dreamily*). The moon's on the rise.

We can hear YEPIKHODOV playing the same gloomy tune as before on his guitar. The moon comes up. Somewhere near the poplars VARYA is looking for Anya and calling, "Anya! Where are you?"

TROFIMOV. Yes, the moon's on the rise.

Pause.

Here's happiness, here it comes, drawing closer and closer, I can already hear its footsteps. And if we don't see it, can't recognize it, what's wrong with that? Others will see it!

VARYA'S VOICE. Anya! Where are you?

TROFIMOV. That Varya again! (*Angrily.*) Aggravating!

ANYA. So what? Let's go down to the river. It's nice there.

TROFIMOV. Let's go.

They leave.

Varya's voice: "Anya! Anya!"

Curtain

ACT THREE

*The drawing-room, separated from the ballroom
by an arch. A chandelier is alight. We can hear a
Jewish orchestra, the same one mentioned in Act
Two, playing in the hallway. Evening. Grand-rond
is being danced in the ballroom. SIMEONOV-
PISHCHIK's voice: "Promenade à une paire!"
The drawing-room is entered by: the first couple
PISHCHIK and CHARLOTTA IVANOVNA, the
second TROFIMOV and LYUBOV ANDREEVNA,
the third ANYA and the POSTAL CLERK, the fourth
VARYA and the STATION MASTER, etc. VARYA
is weeping quietly and, as she dances, wipes away the
tears. In the last couple DUNYASHA. They go around
and through the drawing-room. PISHCHIK calls out:*

"Grand-rond, balançez!" and "Les cavaliers à genoux
et remerciez vos dames!" [53]

FIRS *in a tailcoat crosses the room with a seltzer*
bottle on a tray. PISHCHIK and TROFIMOV enter
the room.

PISHCHIK. I've got high blood pressure, I've already had two strokes, it's tough dancing, but, as the saying goes, when you run with the pack, whether you bark or not, keep on wagging your tail. Actually, I've got the constitution of a horse. My late father, what a card, rest in peace, used to talk of our ancestry as if our venerable line, the Simeonov-Pishchiks, was descended from the very same horse Caligula made a senator . . . [54] (*Sits down.*) But here's the problem: no money! A hungry dog believes only in meat . . . (*Snores and immediately wakes up.*) Just like me . . . I can't think of anything but money . . .

TROFIMOV. As a matter of fact, your build has something horsey about it.

PISHCHIK. So what . . . a horse is a noble beast . . . you could sell a horse . . .

53 Figures in a quadrille: *Promenade à une paire!*: Promenade with your partner! *Grand-rond, balançez!*: reel around, swing your arms! *Les cavaliers à genoux et remerciez vos dames!*: Gentlemen, on your knees and salute your ladies!

54 "To one of his chariot-steeds named Incitatus . . . besides a stable all-built of marble stone for him, and a manger made of ivory, over and above his caparison also and harness of purple . . . he allowed a house and family of servants, yea, and household stuff to furnish the same. . . . It is reported, moreover, that he meant to prefer him into a consulship" (Suetonius, *History of Twelve Caesars*, trans. Philemon Holland [1606]).

We hear billiards played in the next room. VARYA
appears in the archway to the ballroom.

TROFIMOV (*teasing*). Madam Lopakhin! Madam Lopakhin!

VARYA (*angrily*). Scruffy gent!

TROFIMOV. Yes, I'm a scruffy gent and proud of it!

VARYA (*brooding bitterly*). Here we've hired musicians and what
are we going to pay them with? (*Exits.*)

TROFIMOV (*to Pishchik*). If the energy you've wasted in the course
of a lifetime tracking down money to pay off interest had been
harnessed to something else, you probably, ultimately could
have turned the world upside-down.

PISHCHIK. Nietzsche . . . a philosopher . . . the greatest, most
famous . . . a man of immense intellect, says in his works that
it's all right to counterfeit money.

TROFIMOV. So you've read Nietzsche?[55]

PISHCHIK. Well . . . Dashenka told me. But now I'm such straits
that if it came to counterfeiting money . . . Day after tomorrow

---

55 Friedrich Wilhelm Nietzsche (1844–1900), whose philosophy encourages a new
"master" morality for supermen and instigates revolt against the conventional con-
straints of Western civilization in his *Morgenröthe. Gedanken über die moralischen
Vorurtheile* (*Dawns. Reflections on moral prejudices*, 1881). This recalls Chekhov's
statement in a letter (February 25, 1895): "I should like to meet a philosopher like
Nietzsche somewhere on a train or a steamer, and spend the whole night talking to
him. I don't think his philosophy will last very long, though. It's more sensational than
persuasive."

three hundred rubles to pay . . . I've already borrowed a hundred and thirty . . . (*Feeling his pockets, alarmed.*) The money's gone! I've lost the money! (*Through tears.*) Where's the money? (*Gleefully.*) Here it is, in the lining . . . I was really sweating for a minute . . .

Enter LYUBOV ANDREEVNA and
CHARLOTTA IVANOVNA.

LYUBOV ANDREEVNA (*humming a lezginka*).[56] Why is Lyonya taking so long? What's he doing in town? (*To Dunyasha.*) Dunyasha, offer the musicians some tea . . .

TROFIMOV. The auction didn't take place, in all likelihood.

LYUBOV ANDREEVNA. And the musicians showed up at the wrong time and we scheduled the ball for the wrong time . . . Well, never mind . . . (*Sits down and hums softly.*)

CHARLOTTA (*hands Pishchik a deck of cards*). Here's a deck of cards for you, think of a card, any card.

PISHCHIK. I've got one.

CHARLOTTA. Now shuffle the deck. Very good. Hand it over, oh my dear Mister Pishchik. *Ein, zwei, drei!*[57] Now look for it, it's in your side pocket . . .

56 A lively Caucasian dance in two-four time, popularized by Glinka and by Rubinstein in his opera *The Demon.*

57 German: one, two, three.

PISHCHIK (*pulling a card from his side pocket*). Eight of spades, absolutely right! (*Astounded.*) Can you imagine!

CHARLOTTA (*holds deck of cards on her palm, to Trofimov*). Tell me quick, which card's on top?

TROFIMOV. What? Why, the queen of spades.

CHARLOTTA. Right! (*To Pishchik.*) Well? Which card's on top?

PISHCHIK. The ace of hearts.

CHARLOTTA. Right! (*Claps her hand over her palm, the deck of cards disappears.*) Isn't it lovely weather today!

> *She is answered by a mysterious female voice, as if from beneath the floor: "Oh yes, marvelous weather, Madam."*

You're so nice, my ideal . . .

> *Voice: "Madam, I been liking you very much too."*[58]

STATION MASTER (*applauding*). Lady ventriloquist, bravo!

PISHCHIK (*astounded*). Can you imagine! Bewitching Charlotta Ivanovna . . . I'm simply in love with you . . .

CHARLOTTA. In love? (*Shrugging.*) What do you know about love? *Guter Mensch, aber schlechter Musikant.*[59]

---

58 In the Russian, Charlotta confuses her genders, using the masculine singular instead of the feminine plural.

59 German: A good man, but a bad musician. A catchphrase from the comedy *Ponce*

TROFIMOV (*claps Pishchik on the shoulder*). Good old horse . . .

CHARLOTTA. Your attention please, one more trick. (*Takes a laprug from a chair*.) Here is a very nice rug. I'd like to sell it . . . (*Shakes it out.*) What am I offered?

PISHCHIK (*astounded*). Can you imagine!

CHARLOTTA. *Ein, zwei, drei!* (*Quickly lifts the lowered rug.*)

Behind the rug stands ANYA, who curtsies, runs to her mother, embraces her, and runs back to the ballroom amid the general delight.

LYUBOV ANDREEVNA (*applauding*). Bravo, bravo!

CHARLOTTA. One more time! *Ein, zwei, drei!* (*Lifts the rug.*)

Behind the rug stands VARYA, who bows.

PISHCHIK (*astounded*). Can you imagine!

CHARLOTTA. The end! (*Throws the rug at Pishchik, curtsies, and runs into the ballroom.*)

PISHCHIK (*scurrying after her*). You little rascal! . . . How do you like that! How do you like that! (*Exits.*)

LYUBOV ANDREEVNA. And Leonid still isn't back. I don't understand what he can be doing in town all this time! Everything

---

de Leon by Clemens von Brentano (1804), meaning an incompetent, another version of *nedotyopa*.

must be over there, either the estate is sold or the auction didn't take place, but why keep us in suspense so long?

VARYA (*trying to comfort her*). Uncle dear bought it, I'm sure of it.

TROFIMOV (*sarcastically*). Sure.

VARYA. Great-aunt sent him power of attorney, so he could buy it in her name and transfer the debt. She did it for Anya. And I'm sure, God willing, that Uncle dear bought it.

LYUBOV ANDREEVNA. Your great-aunt in Yaroslavl sent fifteen thousand to buy the estate in her name—she doesn't trust us—but that money won't even pay off the interest. (*Hides her face in her hands.*) Today my fate will be decided, my fate . . .

TROFIMOV (*teases Varya*). Madam Lopakhin! Madam Lopakhin!

VARYA (*angrily*). Perpetual student! Twice already you've been expelled from the university.

LYUBOV ANDREEVNA. Why are you getting angry, Varya? He teases you about Lopakhin, what of it? You want to—then marry Lopakhin, he's a good, interesting person. You don't want to—don't get married; darling, nobody's forcing you.

VARYA. I take this seriously, Mama dear, I've got to speak frankly. He's a good man, I like him.

LYUBOV ANDREEVNA. Then marry him. What you're waiting for I cannot understand!

VARYA. Mama dear, I can't propose to him myself. For two years now people have been talking to me about him, everyone's talking, but he either keeps still or cracks jokes. I understand. He's getting rich, busy with his deals, no time for me. If only I'd had some money, even a little, just a hundred rubles, I'd have dropped everything, and gone far away. I'd have entered a convent.

TROFIMOV. Heaven!

VARYA (*to Trofimov*). A student ought to be intelligent! (*In a gentle voice, tearfully.*) You've got so homely, Petya, grown so old! (*To Lyubov Andreevna, no longer weeping.*) Only I can't do without work, Mama dear. I have to have something to do every minute.

Enter YASHA.

YASHA (*can hardly keep from laughing*). Yepikhodov broke a billiard cue!

He exits.

VARYA. What's Yepikhodov doing here? Who gave him permission to play billiards? I don't understand these people . . . (*Exits.*)

LYUBOV ANDREEVNA. Don't tease her, Petya, can't you see she's miserable enough without that?

TROFIMOV. She's just too officious, poking her nose into other people's affairs. All summer long she couldn't leave us in peace, me or Anya, she was afraid a romance might break out. What business is it of hers? And anyway, I didn't show any signs of it, I'm so removed from banality. We're above love!

LYUBOV ANDREEVNA. Well then, I must be beneath love. (*Extremely upset.*) Why isn't Leonid back? If only I knew: is the estate sold or not? Imagining trouble is so hard for me I don't even know what to think, I'm at a loss . . . I could scream right this minute . . . I could do something foolish. Save me, Petya. Say something, tell me . . .

TROFIMOV. Whether the estate's sold today or not—what's the difference? It's been over and done with for a long time now, no turning back, the bridges are burnt. Calm down, dear lady. You mustn't deceive yourself, for once in your life you've got to look the truth straight in the eye.

LYUBOV ANDREEVNA. What truth? You can see where truth is and where falsehood is, but I seem to have lost my sight. I can't see anything. You boldly solve all the major problems, but tell me, dovey, isn't that because you're young, because you haven't had time to suffer through any of your problems? You boldly look forward, but isn't that because you don't see, don't expect anything awful, because life is still hidden from your young eyes? You're more courageous, more sincere, more profound than we are, but stop and think, be indulgent if only in the tips of your fingers, spare me. This is where I was born, after all, this is where my father and my mother lived, my grandfather, I love this house, without the cherry orchard I couldn't make sense of my life, and if it really has to be sold, then sell me along with the orchard . . . (*Embraces Trofimov, kisses him on the forehead.*) Remember, my son was drowned here . . . (*Weeps.*) Show me some pity, dear, kind man.

TROFIMOV. You know I sympathize wholeheartedly.

LYUBOV ANDREEVNA. But you should say so differently, differently . . . (*Takes out a handkerchief, a telegram falls to the floor.*) My heart is so heavy today, you can't imagine. I can't take the noise here, my soul shudders at every sound, I shudder all over, but I can't go off by myself, I'd be terrified to be alone in silence. Don't blame me, Petya . . . I love you like my own flesh and blood. I'd gladly let you marry Anya, believe me, only, dovey, you've got to study, got to finish your degree. You don't do anything, Fate simply tosses you from place to place, it's so odd . . . Isn't that right? Isn't it? And something's got to be done about your beard, to make it grow somehow . . . (*Laughs.*) You look so funny!

TROFIMOV (*picks up the telegram*). I make no claim to be good looking . . .

LYUBOV ANDREEVNA. This telegram's from Paris. Every day I get one. Yesterday too and today. That wild man has fallen ill again, something's wrong with him again . . . He begs my forgiveness, implores me to come back, and actually I ought to go to Paris, stay with him a while. You look so disapproving, Petya, but what's to be done, dovey, what am I to do, he's ill, he's lonely, unhappy, and who's there to look after him, who'll keep him out of mischief, who'll give him his medicine at the right time? And what's there to hide or suppress, I love him, it's obvious, I love him, I love him . . . It's a millstone round my neck, it's dragging me down, but I love that stone and I can't live without it. (*Squeezes Trofimov's hand.*) Don't judge me harshly, Petya, don't say anything, don't talk . . .

TROFIMOV (*through tears*). Forgive my frankness, for God's sake: but he robbed you blind!

LYUBOV ANDREEVNA. No, no, no, you mustn't talk that way . . . (*Covers her ears.*)

TROFIMOV. Why, he's a scoundrel, you're the only one who doesn't realize it! He's a petty scoundrel, a nobody . . .

LYUBOV ANDREEVNA (*getting angry, but under control*). You're twenty-six or twenty-seven, but you're still a sophomoric schoolboy!

TROFIMOV. Is that so?

LYUBOV ANDREEVNA. You should act like a man, at your age you should understand people in love. And you should be in love yourself . . . you should fall in love! (*Angrily.*) Yes, yes! And there's no purity in you, you're simply a puritan, a funny crackpot, a freak . . .

TROFIMOV (*aghast*). What is she saying?

LYUBOV ANDREEVNA. "I am above love!" You're not above love, you're simply, as our Firs says, a half-baked bungler. At your age not to have a mistress! . . .

TROFIMOV (*aghast*). This is horrible! What is she saying! (*Rushes to the ballroom, clutching his head.*) This is horrible . . . I can't stand it, I'm going . . . (*Exits, but immediately returns.*) All is over between us! (*Exits to the hall.*)

LYUBOV ANDREEVNA (*shouting after him*). Petya, wait! You funny man, I was joking! Petya!

> *We hear in the hallway someone running up the stairs and suddenly falling back down with a crash. ANYA and VARYA shriek, but immediately there is the sound of laughter.*

LYUBOV ANDREEVNA. What's going on in there?

> *ANYA runs in.*

ANYA (*laughing*). Petya fell down the stairs! (*Runs out.*)

LYUBOV ANDREEVNA. What a crackpot that Petya is . . .

> *The STATION MASTER stops in the middle of the ballroom and recites Aleksey Tolstoy's "The Sinful Woman."* [60] *The guests listen, but barely has he*

60 Aleksey Konstantinovich Tolstoy (1817–1875), Russian poet; his fustian ballad "*Greshnitsa*" (1858) was frequently recited at public gatherings, and even inspired a painting. It is about a Magdalen and her repentance at a feast in Judaea under the

recited a few lines, when the strains of a waltz reach
them from the hallway, and the recitation breaks off.
Everyone dances. Enter from the hall, TROFIMOV,
ANYA, VARYA, and LYUBOV ANDREEVNA.

Well, Petya . . . well, my pure-in-heart . . . I apologize . . . let's
dance : . . (*Dances with TROFIMOV.*)

ANYA and VARYA dance.

FIRS enters, leaves his stick by the side door. YASHA
also enters the drawing-room, watching the dancers.

YASHA. What's up, Gramps?

FIRS. I'm none too well. In the old days we had generals, bar-
ons, admirals dancing at our parties, but now we send for the
postal clerk and the station master, yes and they don't come
a-running. Somehow I got weak. The late master, the grandfather, doctored everybody with sealing wax for every ailment.
I've took sealing wax every day now for twenty-odd years, and
maybe more, maybe that's why I'm still alive.[61]

---

influence of Christ. Chekhov, who had a low opinion of Tolstoy's poetry, cites it in
his stories to ironic effect. The title refers back to Ranevskaya's catalogue of sins in Act
Two. The opening lines of the poem also comment by contrast on the dowdiness of
her ball:

> The people seethe; joy, laughter flash
> The lute is twanged, the cymbals clash.
> Fern fronds and flowers are strewn about,
> And 'twixt the columns in th'arcade
> In heavy folds the rich brocade
> With ribbon broderie is decked out . . .

61 The treatment is to soak the wax in water, and then drink the water.

YASHA. You bore me stiff, Gramps. (*Yawns.*) How about dropping dead.

FIRS. Eh, you . . . half-baked bungler! (*Mutters.*)

TROFIMOV and LYUBOV ANDREEVNA dance in
the ballroom, then in the drawing-room.

LYUBOV ANDREEVNA. *Merci.* I'm going to sit for a bit . . . (*Sits down.*) I'm tired.

Enter ANYA.

ANYA (*upset*). Just now in the kitchen some man was saying the cherry orchard's been sold already.

LYUBOV ANDREEVNA. Sold to whom?

ANYA. He didn't say. He left. (*Dances with TROFIMOV; they both go into the ballroom.*)

YASHA. There was some old man muttering away. Not one of ours.

FIRS. And Leonid Andreich still isn't back, still not home. That topcoat he's got on's too flimsy, for between seasons, see if he don't catch cold. Eh, when they're young, they're green!

LYUBOV ANDREEVNA. I'll die this instant! Yasha, go and find out to whom it's been sold.

YASHA. He went away a long time ago, that old man. (*Laughs.*)

LYUBOV ANDREEVNA (*somewhat annoyed*). Well, what are you laughing about? What's made you so happy?

YASHA. Yepikhodov's awfully funny. The man's incompetent. Tons of Trouble.

LYUBOV ANDREEVNA. Firs, if the estate is sold, then where will you go?

FIRS. Wherever you order, there I'll go.

LYUBOV ANDREEVNA. Why is your face like that? Aren't you well? You know you ought to be in bed . . .

FIRS. Yes— (*with a grin*) I go to bed, and with me gone, who'll serve, who'll look after things? I'm the only one in the whole house.

YASHA (*to Lyubov Andreevna*). Lyubov Andreevna! Let me ask you a favor, be so kind! If you go off to Paris again, take me with you, please. For me to stick around here is absolutely out of the question. (*Glances around, lowers his voice.*) It goes without saying, you can see for yourself, the country's uncivilized, the people are immoral, not to mention the boredom, in the kitchen they feed us garbage and there's that Firs going around, muttering all kinds of improper remarks. Take me with you, be so kind!

Enter PISHCHIK.

PISHCHIK. May I request . . . a teeny waltz, loveliest of ladies . . . (*LYUBOV ANDREEVNA goes with him.*) Enchanting lady, I'll borrow a hundred and eighty little rubles off you just the same . . . Yes, I will . . . (*Dances.*) A hundred and eighty little rubles . . .

They have passed into the ballroom.

YASHA (*singing softly*). "Wilt thou learn my soul's unrest . . ."[62]

*In the ballroom a figure in a gray top hat and checked
trousers waves its arms and jumps up and down;
shouts of "Bravo, Charlotta Ivanovna!"*

DUNYASHA (*stops to powder her nose*). The young mistress orders
me to dance—lots of gentlemen and few ladies—but dancing makes my head swim, my heart pound, Firs Nikolaevich,
and just now the postal clerk told me something that took my
breath away.

Music subsides.

FIRS. Well, what did he tell you?

DUNYASHA. You, he says, are like a flower.

YASHA (*yawns*). How uncouth . . . (*Exits.*)

DUNYASHA. Like a flower . . . I'm such a sensitive girl, I'm
awfully fond of compliments.

FIRS. You'll get your head turned.

Enter YEPIKHODOV.

YEPIKHODOV. Avdotya Fyodorovna, you don't wish to see
me . . . as if I were some sort of bug. (*Sighs.*) Ech, life!

DUNYASHA. What can I do for you?

---

62 Title and opening line of a ballad by N. S. Rzhevskaya (1869).

YEPIKHODOV. Indubitably you may be right. (*Sighs.*) But, of course, if it's considered from a standpoint, then you, if I may venture the expression, pardon my outspokenness, positively drove me into a state of mind. I know my lot, every day I run into some kind of trouble, and I've grown accustomed to that long ago, so I look upon my destiny with a smile. You gave me your word, and even though I . . .

DUNYASHA. Please, let's talk later on, but leave me alone for now. I'm dreaming now. (*Toys with her fan.*)

YEPIKHODOV. Every day I run into trouble, and I, if I may venture the expression, merely smile, even laugh.

Enter VARYA from the ballroom.

VARYA. Haven't you gone yet, Semyon? Honestly, you are the most disrespectful man. (*To Dunyasha.*) Clear out of here, Dunyasha. (*To Yepikhodov.*) If you're not playing billiards and breaking the cue, you're lounging around the drawing-room like a guest.

YEPIKHODOV. To take me to task, if I may venture the expression, you can't.

VARYA. I'm not taking you to task, I'm just telling you. But you know all you do is walk around instead of attending to business. We keep a bookkeeper but nobody knows what for.

YEPIKHODOV (*offended*). Whether I work or whether I walk or whether I eat or whether I play billiards may be criticized only by my elders and betters who know what they're talking about.

VARYA. How dare you say such things to me! (*Flying into a rage.*) How dare you? You mean I don't know what I'm talking about? Get out of here! This minute!

YEPIKHODOV (*alarmed*). Please express yourself in a more refined manner.

VARYA (*beside herself*). This very minute, out of here! Out! (*He goes to the door, she follows him.*) Tons of Trouble! Don't draw another breath here! Don't let me set eyes on you!

> YEPIKHODOV *has gone, behind the door his voice:*
> "*I'm going to complain about you.*"

So, you're coming back? (*Seizes the stick Firs left near the door.*) Come on . . . come on . . . come on, I'll show you . . . Well, are you coming? Are you coming? Here's what you get . . . (*Swings the stick.*)

> At the same moment, LOPAKHIN enters.

LOPAKHIN. My humble thanks.

VARYA (*angrily and sarcastically*). Sorry!

LOPAKHIN. Never mind, ma'am. Thank you kindly for the pleasant surprise.

VARYA. Don't mention it. (*Starts out, then looks back and asks gently.*) I didn't hurt you?

LOPAKHIN. No, it's nothing. The bump is going to be enormous, though.

> *Voices in the ballroom: "Lopakhin's here, Yermolay Alekseich!"*

PISHCHIK. Sights to be seen, sounds to be heard . . . (*He and LOPAKHIN exchange kisses.*) There's cognac on your breath, my dear boy, apple of my eye. But we were making merry here too.

> *Enter LYUBOV ANDREEVNA.*

LYUBOV ANDREEVNA. Is that you, Yermolay Alekseich? Why the delay? Where's Leonid?

LOPAKHIN. Leonid Andreich came back with me, he's on his way . . .

LYUBOV ANDREEVNA (*agitated*). Well, what? Was there an auction? Say something!

LOPAKHIN (*embarrassed, afraid to reveal his glee*). The auction was over by four o'clock . . . We missed the train, had to wait till half-past nine. (*Sighs heavily.*) Oof! My head's a little woozy . . .

> *Enter GAEV; his right hand is holding packages, his left is wiping away tears.*

LYUBOV ANDREEVNA. Lyonya, what? Well, Lyonya? (*Impatiently, tearfully.*) Hurry up, for God's sake . . .

GAEV (*not answering her, only waves his hand to Firs, weeping*). Here, take this . . . There's anchovies, smoked herring . . . I haven't had a thing to eat all day . . . What I've been through!

> *The door to the billiard room opens. We hear the click of the balls and YASHA's voice: "Seven and eighteen!" GAEV's expression alters, he stops crying.*

I'm awfully tired. Firs, help me change. (*Exits through the ballroom, followed by FIRS.*)

PISHCHIK. What about the auction? Tell us!

LYUBOV ANDREEVNA. Is the cherry orchard sold?

LOPAKHIN. Sold.

LYUBOV ANDREEVNA. Who bought it?

LOPAKHIN. I bought it.

> *Pause. LYUBOV ANDREEVNA is overcome; she would fall, were she not standing beside an armchair and a table. VARYA removes the keys from her belt, throws them on the floor in the middle of the drawing room and exits.*

LOPAKHIN. I bought it! Wait, ladies and gentlemen, do me a favor, my head's swimming, I can't talk . . . (*Laughs.*) We got to the auction, Deriganov's there already. Leonid Andreich only had fifteen thousand, and right off Deriganov bid thirty over and above the mortgage. I get the picture, I pitched into him, bid forty. He forty-five, I fifty-five. I mean, he kept upping it by fives, I by tens . . . Well, it ended. Over and above the mortgage I bid ninety thousand, it was knocked down to me. Now the cherry orchard's mine. Mine! (*Chuckling.*) My God, Lord, the cherry orchard's mine! Tell me I'm drunk, out of my mind, that I'm making it all up . . . (*Stamps his feet.*) Don't laugh at me! If only my father and grandfather could rise up from their graves and see all that's happened, how their Yermolay, beaten, barely literate Yermolay, who used to run around barefoot in the wintertime; how this same Yermolay bought the estate, the most beautiful thing in the world. I bought the estate where my grandfather and father were slaves, where they weren't even allowed in the kitchen. I'm dreaming, it's a halluci- nation, it only looks this way . . . This is a figment of your imagination, veiled by shadows of obscurity . . .[63] (*Picks up the keys, smiles gently.*) She threw down the keys, she wants to show that she's no longer in charge here . . . (*Jingles the keys.*) Well, it doesn't matter.

We hear the orchestra tuning up.

Hey, musicians, play, I want to hear you! Come on, everybody, see how Yermolay Lopakhin will swing an axe in the cherry orchard, how the trees'll come tumbling to the ground! We'll

---

63 George Calderon states that this is "a cant jocular phrase, a literary tag. Lopakhin is quoting out of some bad play, as usual when he is lively." Chekhov uses it in his correspondence.

build cottages, and our grandchildren and great-grandchildren will see a new life here . . . Music, play!

*The music plays, LYUBOV ANDREEVNA has sunk
into a chair, crying bitterly.*

(*Reproachfully.*) Why, oh, why didn't you listen to me? My poor, dear lady, you can't undo it now. (*Tearfully.*) Oh, if only this were all over quickly, if somehow our ungainly, unhappy life could be changed quickly.

PISHCHIK (*takes him by the arm; in an undertone*). She's crying. Let's go into the ballroom, leave her alone . . . Let's go . . . (*Drags him by the arm and leads him into the ballroom.*)

LOPAKHIN. So what? Music, play in tune! Let everything be the way I want it! (*Ironically.*) Here comes the new landlord, the owner of the cherry orchard! (*He accidentally bumps into a small table and almost knocks over the candelabrum.*) I can pay for everything!

Exits with PISHCHIK.

*No one is left in the ballroom or drawing-room except
LYUBOV ANDREEVNA, who is sitting, all hunched
up, weeping bitterly. The music is playing softly.
ANYA and TROFIMOV hurry in. ANYA goes to her
mother and kneels before her. TROFIMOV remains at
the entrance to the ballroom.*

ANYA. Mama! . . . Mama, you're crying? Dear, kind, good Mama, my own, my beautiful, I love you . . . I bless you. The cherry orchard's sold, it's gone now, that's true, true, true, but don't cry, Mama, you've still got your life ahead of you, you've still got your good pure heart . . . Come with me, come, dearest, let's go away from here, let's go! . . . We'll plant a new orchard, more splendid than this one, you'll see it, you'll understand, and joy, peaceful, profound joy will sink into your heart, like the sun when night falls, and you'll smile, Mama! Let's go, dearest! Let's go! . . .

Curtain

ACT FOUR

First act setting. Neither curtains on the windows
nor pictures on the wall, a few sticks of furniture
remain, piled up in a corner as if for sale. A feeling
of emptiness. Near the door to the outside and at
the back of the stage are piles of suitcases, traveling
bags, etc. The door at left is open, and through
it we can hear the voices of Varya and Anya.
LOPAKHIN stands, waiting. YASHA is holding a
tray of glasses filled with champagne. In the hallway,

*YEPIKHODOV is tying up a carton. Offstage, at the
back, a murmur. It's the peasants come to say good-
bye. GAEV's voice: "Thank you, friends, thank you."*

YASHA. The common folk have come to say good-bye. I'm of the
opinion, Yermolay Alekseich, they're decent enough people,
but not very bright.

*The murmur subsides. Enter through the hall
LYUBOV ANDREEVNA and GAEV. She isn't
crying, but is pale, her face twitches, she can't talk.*

GAEV. You gave them your purse, Lyuba. You shouldn't have!
You shouldn't have!

LYUBOV ANDREEVNA. I couldn't help it! I couldn't help it!

They go out.

LOPAKHIN (*through the door, after them*). Please, I humbly beseech
you! A little drink at parting! It didn't occur to me to bring any
from town, and at the station I only found one bottle. Please!

Pause.

How about it, ladies and gentlemen? Don't you want any?
(*Walks away from the door.*) If I'd known, I wouldn't have
bought it. Well, I won't drink any either.

YASHA carefully sets the tray on a chair.

Drink up, Yasha, you have some.

YASHA. Greetings to those departing!⁶⁴ And happy days to the stay-at-homes! (*Drinks.*) This champagne isn't the genuine article, you can take it from me.

LOPAKHIN. Eight rubles a bottle.

Pause.

It's cold as hell in here.

YASHA. They didn't stoke up today, it doesn't matter, we're leaving. (*Laughs.*)

LOPAKHIN. What's that for?

YASHA. Sheer satisfaction.

LOPAKHIN. Outside it's October, but sunny and mild, like summer. Good building weather. (*Glances at his watch, at the door.*) Ladies and gentlemen, remember, until the train leaves, there's forty-six minutes in all! Which means, in twenty minutes we start for the station. Get a move on.

Enter from outdoors TROFIMOV in an overcoat.

TROFIMOV. Seems to me it's time to go now. The horses are at the door. Where the hell are my galoshes? Disappeared. (*Through the door.*) Anya, my galoshes aren't here! I can't find them!

---

64 Yasha is distorting a phrase usually applied to welcome arrivals.

LOPAKHIN. And I have to be in Kharkov. I'll go with you on the same train. I'm spending all winter in Kharkov. I've been hanging around here with you, I'm worn out with nothing to do. I've got to be doing something, I don't even know where to put my hands; they dangle this funny way, like somebody else's.

TROFIMOV. We'll be going soon, and you can return to your productive labors.

LOPAKHIN. Do have a little drink.

TROFIMOV. None for me.

LOPAKHIN. In other words, back to Moscow now?

TROFIMOV. Yes, I'll go with them as far as town, but tomorrow back to Moscow.

LOPAKHIN. Yes . . . Hey, the professors are on a lecture strike, I'll bet they're waiting for you to show up!

TROFIMOV. None of your business.

LOPAKHIN. How many years have you been studying at the University?

TROFIMOV. Think up something fresher. That's old and stale. (*Looks for his galoshes.*) You know, it's unlikely we'll ever meet again, so let me give you a piece of advice as a farewell: don't wave your arms! Break yourself of that habit—arm-waving. And cottage-building as well, figuring that vacationers will eventually turn into property owners, figuring that way is just the same as arm-waving . . . Anyhow, I can't help liking you. You've got delicate, gentle fingers, like an artist, you've got a delicate, gentle heart . . . [65]

LOPAKHIN (*hugs him*). Good-bye, my boy. Thanks for everything. If you need it, borrow some money from me for the trip.

TROFIMOV. What for? Don't need it.

LOPAKHIN. But you don't have any!

TROFIMOV. I do. Thank you. I got some for a translation. Here it is, in my pocket. (*Anxiously.*) But my galoshes are missing!

VARYA (*from the next room*). Take your nasty things! (*She flings a pair of rubber galoshes on stage.*)

TROFIMOV. What are you upset about, Varya? Hm . . . But these aren't my galoshes!

LOPAKHIN. Last spring I planted nearly three thousand acres of poppies, and now I've cleared forty thousand net. And when my poppies bloomed, it was like a picture! So look, what I'm getting at is, I cleared forty thousand, which means I offer you

65 These lines did not exist in the first version of the play but were added to support Chekhov's view of Lopakhin as a decent person.

a loan because I can afford it. Why turn up your nose? I'm a peasant . . . plain and simple.

TROFIMOV. Your father was a peasant, mine a druggist, and it all adds up to absolutely nothing.

LOPAKHIN pulls out his wallet.

Don't bother, don't bother . . . Even if you gave me two hundred thousand, I wouldn't take it. I'm a free man. And everything that you all value so highly and fondly, rich men and beggars alike, hasn't the slightest effect on me, it's like fluff floating in the air. I can manage without you, I can pass you by, I'm strong and proud. Humanity is moving toward the most sublime truth, the most sublime happiness possible on earth, and I'm in the front ranks!

LOPAKHIN. Will you get there?

TROFIMOV. I'll get there.

Pause.

I'll get there, or I'll blaze a trail for others to get there.

We hear in the distance an axe striking a tree.

LOPAKHIN. Well, good-bye, my boy. Time to go. We turn up our noses at one another, while life keeps slipping by. When I work a long time nonstop, then my thoughts are clearer, and I even seem to know why I exist. But, pal, how many people there are in Russia who don't know why they exist. Well, what's the difference, that's not what makes the world go round. Leonid Andreich, they say, took a job, he'll be in the bank, six thousand a year . . . Only he won't keep at it, too lazy . . .

ANYA (*in the doorway*). Mama begs you: until she's gone, not to chop down the orchard.

TROFIMOV. I mean really, haven't you got any tact . . . (*Exits through the hall.*)

LOPAKHIN. Right away, right away . . . These people, honestly! (*Exits after him.*)

ANYA. Did they take Firs to the hospital?

YASHA. I told them to this morning. They took him, I should think.

ANYA (*to Yepikhodov, who is crossing through the room*). Semyon Panteleich, please find out whether Firs was taken to the hospital.

YASHA (*offended*). I told Yegor this morning. Why ask a dozen times?

YEPIKHODOV. Superannuated Firs, in my conclusive opinion, is past all repairing, he should be gathered to his fathers. And I can only envy him. (*Sets a suitcase on top of a cardboard hatbox and crushes it.*) Well, look at that, typical. I should have known.

YASHA (*scoffing*). Tons of Trouble . . .

YEPIKHODOV. Well, it could have happened to anybody.[66] (*Exits.*)

VARYA (*from behind the door*). Have they sent Firs to the hospital?

ANYA. They have.

VARYA. Then why didn't they take the letter to the doctor?

ANYA. We'll have to send someone after them . . . (*Exits.*)

VARYA (*from the next room*). Where's Yasha? Tell him his mother's here, wants to say good-bye to him.

YASHA (*waves his hand in dismissal*). They simply try my patience.

> DUNYASHA *in the meantime has been fussing with the luggage; now that* YASHA *is alone, she comes up to him.*

DUNYASHA. If only you'd take one little look at me, Yasha. You're going away . . . you're leaving me behind . . . (*Weeps and throws herself on his neck.*)

YASHA. What's the crying for? (*Drinks champagne.*) In six days I'll be in Paris again. Tomorrow we'll board an express train and

---

66 This line does not appear in any of the printed editions but was improvised in performance by Ivan Moskvin. It got a laugh, and he asked if he could keep it in. "Tell Moskvin he can insert the new new lines, and I will put them in myself when I read the corrected proofs. I give him the most complete carte blanche" (Chekhov to Olga Knipper, March 20, 1904). Somehow, Chekhov never did insert the line in the proofs, but it appears penciled in to the Moscow Art Theatre prompt script.

dash away, we'll be gone in a flash. Somehow I can't believe it. Veev lah Franz! . . . It doesn't suit me here, I can't live . . . nothing going on. I've had an eyeful of uncouth behavior—I'm fed up with it. (*Drinks champagne.*) What's the crying for? Behave respectably, then you won't have to cry.[67]

DUNYASHA (*powdering her nose, looks in a hand mirror*). Drop me a line from Paris. I really loved you, Yasha, loved you so! I'm a soft-hearted creature, Yasha!

YASHA. Someone's coming in here. (*Fusses with the luggage, humming softly.*)

Enter LYUBOV ANDREEVNA, GAEV, ANYA, and
CHARLOTTA IVANOVNA.

GAEV. We should be off. Not much time left. (*Looking at Yasha.*) Who's that smelling of herring?

LYUBOV ANDREEVNA. In about ten minutes we ought to be getting into the carriages. (*Casting a glance round the room.*) Good-bye, dear old house, old grandfather. Winter will pass, spring will come again, but you won't be here anymore, they'll tear you down. How much these walls have seen! (*Kissing her daughter ardently.*) My precious, you're radiant, your eyes are sparkling like two diamonds. Are you happy? Very?

---

67 Another echo of Hamlet to Ophelia: "If you are honest and fair, your honesty could admit no props to your fairness" (Act II, scene 1).

ANYA. Very! A new life is beginning, Mama!

GAEV (*gaily*). As a matter of fact, everything's fine now. Before the sale of the cherry orchard, we were all upset, distressed, but then, once the matter was settled finally, irrevocably, everyone calmed down, even cheered up . . . I'm a bank employee, now I'm a financier . . . yellow to the center, and you, Lyuba, anyway, you're looking better, that's for sure.

LYUBOV ANDREEVNA. Yes. My nerves are better, that's true.

They help her on with her hat and coat.

I sleep well. Carry my things out, Yasha. It's time. (*To Anya.*) My little girl, we'll be back together soon . . . I'm off to Paris, I'll live there on that money your great-aunt in Yaroslavl sent us to buy the estate — hurray for Auntie! — but that money won't last long.

ANYA. Mama, you'll come back soon, soon . . . won't you? I'll study, pass the finals at the high school and then I'll work to help you. Mama, we'll be together and read all sorts of books . . . Won't we? (*Kisses her mother's hand.*) We'll read in the autumn evenings, we'll read lots of books, and before us a new, wonderful world will open up . . . (*Dreamily.*) Mama, come back . . .

LYUBOV ANDREEVNA. I'll come back, my precious. (*Embraces her daughter.*)

Enter LOPAKHIN. CHARLOTTA is quietly singing a song.

GAEV. Charlotta's happy! She's singing!

CHARLOTTA (*picks up a bundle that looks like a swaddled baby*). Rock-a-bye, baby, on the tree top . . .

We hear a baby crying: "Waa! Waa!"

Hush, my sweet, my dear little boy.

"Waa! . . . Waa! . . ."

I'm so sorry for you! (*Throws down the bundle.*) Will you please find me a position. I can't keep on this way.

LOPAKHIN. We'll find one, Charlotta Ivanovna, don't worry.

GAEV. Everyone's dropping us, Varya's leaving . . . we've suddenly become superfluous.

CHARLOTTA. There's nowhere for me to live in town. Have to go away . . . (*Hums.*) What difference does it make?

Enter PISHCHIK.

LOPAKHIN. The freak of nature!

PISHCHIK (*out of breath*). Oy, let me catch my breath . . . I'm winded . . . my most honored . . . Give me some water . . .

GAEV. After money, I suppose? Your humble servant, deliver me from temptation . . . (*Exits.*)

PISHCHIK (*out of breath*). I haven't been to see you for the longest time . . . loveliest of ladies . . . (*To Lopakhin.*) You here . . . glad to see you . . . a man of the most enormous intellect . . . take . . . go on . . . (*Hands money to Lopakhin.*) Four hundred rubles . . . I still owe you eight hundred and forty . . .

LOPAKHIN (*bewildered, shrugs*). It's like a dream . . . Where did you get this?

PISHCHIK. Wait . . . Hot . . . Most amazing thing happened. Some Englishmen[68] stopped by my place and found on my land some kind of white clay . . . (*To Lyubov Andreevna.*) And four hundred for you . . . beautiful lady, divine creature . . . (*Hands her money.*) The rest later. (*Drinks water.*) Just now some young man on the train was telling about some sort of . . . great philosopher who recommends jumping off roofs . . . "Jump!"—he says, and that solves the whole problem. (*Astounded.*) Can you imagine! Water! . . .

LOPAKHIN. Who were these Englishmen?

PISHCHIK. I leased them the lot with the clay for twenty-four years . . . But now, excuse me, no time . . . Have to run along . . . I'm going to Znoikov's . . . Kardamonov's . . . I owe everybody . . . (*Drinks.*) Your good health . . . On Thursday I'll drop by . . .

LYUBOV ANDREEVNA. We're just about to move to town, and tomorrow I'll be abroad.

---

68 The British often appear in nineteenth-century Russian fiction as progressive and enterprising businessmen. They were often hired as estate managers, land surveyors, or experts in animal husbandry. The uncle of the writer Nikolay Leskov was a Scotsman who managed several vast Russian estates for their aristocratic owners.

PISHCHIK. What? (*Agitated.*) Why to town? Goodness, look at the furniture . . . the suitcases . . . well, never mind . . . (*Through tears.*) Never mind. Persons of the highest intelligence . . . those Englishmen . . . Never mind . . . Be happy . . . God will come to your aid . . . Never mind . . . Everything in this world comes to an end . . . (*Kisses Lyubov Andreevna's hand.*) And should rumor reach you that my end has come, just remember this very thing—a horse, and say: "Once there lived an old so-and-so . . . Simeonov-Pishchik . . . rest in peace" . . . The most incredible weather . . . yes . . . (*Exits, overcome with emotion, but immediately reappears in the doorway and says:*) Dashenka sends you her regards! (*Exits.*)

LYUBOV ANDREEVNA. Now we can go. I'm leaving with two things on my mind. First—that Firs is ill. (*Glancing at her watch.*) There's still five minutes . . .

ANYA. Mama, they've already sent Firs to the hospital. Yasha sent him this morning.

LYUBOV ANDREEVNA. My second anxiety is Varya. She's used to rising early and working, and now, without work, she's like a fish out of water. She's lost weight, she's got pale, she cries, poor soul . . .

Pause.

You know this perfectly well, Yermolay Alekseich; I had dreamt . . . of marrying her to you, yes, and it certainly looked as if you were going to get married. (*Whispers to Anya, who nods to Charlotta, and both leave.*) She loves you, you're fond of her, I don't know, I just don't know why you seem to sidestep one another. I don't understand!

LOPAKHIN. I don't understand either, I admit. It's all strange somehow . . . If there's still time, then I'm ready right now . . . Let's get it over with right away—and that'll be that, but if it wasn't for you, I have the feeling I wouldn't be proposing.

LYUBOV ANDREEVNA. That's wonderful. One little minute is all it takes. I'll call her right now . . .

LOPAKHIN. And there's champagne for the occasion. (*Looks in the glasses.*) Empty, somebody drank it already.

YASHA coughs.

I should say, lapped it up . . .

LYUBOV ANDREEVNA (*lively*). Fine! We'll go outside . . . Yasha, *allez!*[69] I'll call her . . . (*In the doorway.*) Varya, drop everything, come here. Come on! (*Exits with YASHA.*)

LOPAKHIN (*glancing at his watch.*) Yes . . .

Pause.

*Behind the door a stifled laugh, whispering, finally
VARYA enters.*

VARYA (*inspects the luggage for a long time*). That's funny, I just can't find it . . .

---

69 French: go on!

LOPAKHIN. What are you looking for?

VARYA. I packed it myself and can't remember.

Pause.

LOPAKHIN. Where are you off to now, Varvara Mikhailovna?

VARYA. Me? To the Ragulins' . . . I've agreed to take charge of their household . . . as a housekeeper, sort of.

LOPAKHIN. That's in Yashnevo? About fifty miles from here.

Pause.

So ends life in this house . . .

VARYA (*examining the luggage*). Where in the world is it . . . Or maybe I packed it in the trunk . . . Yes, life in this house is over . . . there won't be any more . . .

LOPAKHIN. And I'll be riding to Kharkov soon . . . by the same train. Lots of business. But I'm leaving Yepikhodov on the grounds . . . I hired him.

VARYA. Is that so!

LOPAKHIN. Last year by this time it was already snowing, if you remember, but now it's mild, sunny. Except that it's cold . . . About three degrees of frost.

VARYA. I haven't noticed.

Pause.

And besides our thermometer is broken . . .

Pause.

*Voice from outside through the door: "Yermolay
Alekseich!"*

LOPAKHIN (*as if expecting this call for a long time*). Right away!
(*Rushes out.*)

*VARYA, sitting on the floor, laying her head on a pile
of dresses, quietly sobs. The door opens, LYUBOV
ANDREEVNA enters cautiously.*

LYUBOV ANDREEVNA. Well?

Pause.

We've got to go.

VARYA (*has stopped crying, wipes her eyes*). Yes, it's time, Mama
dear. I'll get to the Ragulins' today, provided I don't miss the
train . . .

LYUBOV ANDREEVNA (*in the doorway*). Anya, put your things
on!

*Enter ANYA, then GAEV, CHARLOTTA
IVANOVNA. GAEV has on a heavy overcoat
with a hood. The servants and coachmen gather.
YEPIKHODOV fusses around the luggage.*

Now we can be on our way.

ANYA (*joyously*). On our way!

GAEV. My friends, my dearly beloved friends! Abandoning this house forever, can I be silent, can I refrain from expressing at parting those feelings which now fill my whole being . . .

ANYA (*entreating*). Uncle! . . .

VARYA. Uncle dear, you mustn't!

GAEV (*downcast*). Bank the yellow to the center . . . I'll keep still . . .

Enter TROFIMOV, then LOPAKHIN.

TROFIMOV. Well, ladies and gentlemen, time to go!

LOPAKHIN. Yepikhodov, my overcoat!

LYUBOV ANDREEVNA. I'll sit just one little minute.[70] It's as if I never saw before what the walls in this house are like, what the ceilings are like, and now I gaze at them greedily, with such tender love . . .

GAEV. I remember when I was six, on Trinity Sunday[71] I sat in this window and watched my father driving to church . . .

LYUBOV ANDREEVNA. Is all the luggage loaded?

---

70 Sitting down for a brief while before leaving for a journey was an old Russian custom.

71 Pentecost or Whitsunday, always the Sunday that is closest to fifty days from Russian Easter.

LOPAKHIN. Everything, I think. (*Putting on his overcoat, to Yepik-hodov.*) You there, Yepikhodov, see that everything's in order.

YEPIKHODOV (*in a hoarse voice*). Don't worry, Yermolay Alekseich!

LOPAKHIN. What's the matter with you?

YEPIKHODOV. I just drank some water, swallowed something.

YASHA (*contemptuously*). How uncouth . . .

LYUBOV ANDREEVNA. We're going—and there won't be a soul left here.

LOPAKHIN. Not until spring.

VARYA (*pulls a parasol out of a bundle, looking as if she were about to hit someone*).

LOPAKHIN *pretends to be scared.*

What are you, what are you doing . . . it never entered my mind . . .

TROFIMOV. Ladies and gentlemen, let's get into the car-riages . . . It's high time! The train'll be here any minute!

VARYA. Petya, here they are, your galoshes, next to the suitcase. (*Tearfully.*) And yours are so muddy, so old . . .

TROFIMOV (*putting on his galoshes*). Let's go, ladies and gentle-men!

GAEV (*overcome with emotion, afraid he'll cry*). The train . . . the station . . . Follow-shot to the center, white doublette to the corner . . .

LYUBOV ANDREEVNA. Let's go!

LOPAKHIN. Everybody here? Nobody there? (*Locking the side door at the left.*) Things stored here, have to lock up. Let's go! . . .

ANYA. Good-bye, house! Good-bye, old life!

TROFIMOV. Hello, new life! (*Exits with ANYA.*)

> VARYA *casts a glance around the room and exits unhurriedly. YASHA and CHARLOTTA with her lapdog go out.*

LOPAKHIN. Which means, till spring. Come along, ladies and gentlemen . . . Till we meet again! . . . (*Exits.*)

> LYUBOV ANDREEVNA *and GAEV are left alone. As if they had been waiting for this, they throw their arms around one another's neck and sob with restraint, quietly, afraid of being heard.*

GAEV (*in despair*). Sister dear, sister dear . . .

LYUBOV ANDREEVNA. Oh, my darling, my sweet, beautiful orchard! . . . My life, my youth, my happiness, good-bye! . . . Good-bye! . . .

ANYA's voice (gaily, appealing): "Mama! . . ."

TROFIMOV's voice (gaily, excited): "Yoo-hoo! . . ."

LYUBOV ANDREEVNA. One last look at the walls, the windows . . . Our poor mother loved to walk in this room . . .

GAEV. Sister dear, sister dear! . . .

ANYA's voice: "Mama! . . ."

TROFIMOV's voice: "Yoo-hoo! . . ."

LYUBOV ANDREEVNA. We're coming! . . .

They go out.

The stage is empty. We hear all the doors being locked with a key, and then the carriages driving off. It grows quiet. In the stillness there is the dull thud of an axe against a tree, sounding forlorn and dismal.

We hear footsteps. From the door at right FIRS appears. He's dressed as always, in a jacket and white waistcoat, slippers on his feet. He is ill.

FIRS (*crosses to the door, tries the knob*). Locked. They've gone . . . (*Sits on the sofa.*) Forgot about me . . . Never mind . . . I'll sit here a spell . . . And Leonid Andreich, I'll bet, didn't put on his fur coat, went out in his topcoat . . . (*Sighs, anxiously.*) I didn't see to it . . . When they're young, they're green! (*Mutters something that cannot be understood.*) This life's gone by like I ain't lived. (*Lies down.*) I'll lie down a

spell . . . Not a bit o' strength left in you, nothing left, nothing . . . Eh you . . . half-baked bungler! . . . (*Lies immobile.*)

*We hear the distant sound, as if from the sky, the
sound of a breaking string, dying away mournfully.
Silence ensues, and all we hear far away in the
orchard is the thud of an axe on a tree.*

Curtain

VARIANTS

Lines come from the original manuscript version (A1), a subsequent set of corrections (A2), the manuscript with the addition to Act Two (AA), and the first publication in the anthology *Knowledge* (*Znanie*) (K).

ACT ONE

page 79 / *Replace*: Everyone talks about our getting married . . . it's all like a dream . . .

with: Everyone talks about our getting married, everyone offers congratulations, and he looks just as if he was about to propose any minute now, but in fact there's nothing to it, it's all like a dream, an unsettling, bad dream . . . Sometimes it even gets scary, I don't know what to do with myself . . . (A2)

page 86 / *Replace*: I'd like to tell you . . . Here's my plan.

with: This is what I want to say before I go. (*After a glance at his watch.*) Now about the estate . . . in two words . . . I want to propose to you a means of finding a way out. So that your estate doesn't incur losses, you'd have to get up every day at four in the morning and work all day long. For you, of course, that's impossible, I understand . . . But there is another way out. (A1)

page 91 / *Replace*: Nothing doing. I want to go to bed. (*Exits.*)

with: (*walking over to the door*). Who is that standing in the doorway? Who's there? (*Knock on the door from that side.*) Who's that knocking? (*Knock.*) That gentleman is my fiancé. (*Exits.*) *Everyone laughs.* (A1 & 2)

page 92 / *After*: He's a good man. — By the way, how much do we owe him?

GAEV. For the second mortgage just a trifle—about forty thousand. (A1)

Stage direction: a peaceful mood has returned to her, she is happy. (A1 & 2)

ACT TWO

page 102 / *Opening stage direction: YASHA and DUNYASHA are sitting on a bench, YEPIKHODOV stands nearby. From the estate along the road TROFIMOV and ANYA pass by.*

ANYA. Great Aunt lives alone, she's very rich. She doesn't like Mamma. At first it was hard for me staying with her, she didn't talk much to me. Then nothing, she relented. She promised to send the money, gave me and Charlotta Ivanovna something for the trip. But how awful, how hard it is to feel that one is a poor relation.

TROFIMOV. There's somebody here already, it looks like . . . They're sitting down. In that case, let's walk along a little farther.

ANYA. Three weeks I've been away from home. I missed it so much!

They leave. (A1 & 2)

page 106 / *After:* Tasty little pickle! — *Pause.* (A2, AA)

page 106 / *After:* a girl who misbehaves . . . — (*Sings quietly, and because he has no ear, extremely off-key*) "Would you know my soul's unrest." (A2)

page 106 / *After:* The masters . . . — (*Rapidly.*) Come here today when it gets dark. Be sure to come . . . (A1 & 2)

page 110 / *After:* Maybe we'll think of something. —
VARYA and CHARLOTTA IVANOVNA pass by on the road from the estate. CHARLOTTA is in a man's cap with a gun.

VARYA. She's an intelligent, well-bred girl, nothing can happen, but all the same it's not right to leave her alone with a young man. Supper's at nine, Charlotta Ivanovna.

CHARLOTTA. I don't want to eat. (*Quietly hums a ditty.*)

VARYA. It doesn't matter. You have to for decency's sake. There, you see, they're sitting there on the riverbank . . .

    VARYA and CHARLOTTA leave. (A1 & 2)

page 113 / *After:* (*Inspects him.*) — Today should be the light-weight gray suit, but this one's a disgrace. (A1)

page 118 / *After:* **ANYA** (*dreamily*). There goes Yepikhodov . . . —

VARYA. How come he's living with us? He only eats on the run and drinks tea all day long . . .

LOPAKHIN. And makes plans to shoot himself.

LYUBOV ANDREEVNA. But I love Yepikhodov. When he talks about his troubles, it gets so funny. Don't discharge him, Varya.

VARYA. There's no other way, Mamma dear. We have to discharge him, the good-for-nothing. (A2)

page 124 / *Replace:* **TROFIMOV.** Believe me, Anya, believe! . . . **Curtain**

with: **TROFIMOV.** Tsss . . . Someone's coming. That Varya again! (*Angrily.*) Exasperating!

ANYA. So what? Let's go to the river. It's nice there . . .

TROFIMOV. Let's go . . .

    They start out.

ANYA. Soon the moon will rise.

    They leave.

    Enter FIRS, then CHARLOTTA IVANOVNA. FIRS,
    muttering, is looking for something on the ground near
    the bench, lights a match.

CHARLOTTA. That you, Firs? What are you up to?

FIRS (*mutters*). Eh, you half-baked bungler!

CHARLOTTA (*sits on the bench and removes her cap*). That you, Firs? What are you looking for?

FIRS. Mistress mislaid her purse.

CHARLOTTA (*looking*). Here's a fan . . . And here's a hanky . . . smells of perfume.

Pause.

Nothing else. Lyubov Andreevna is constantly mislaying things. She's even mislaid her own life. (*Quietly sings a little song.*) I haven't got a valid passport, Granddad, I don't know how old I am, and I always feel like I'm still oh so young . . . (*Puts her cap on Firs; he sits motionless.*) O, I love you, my dear sir! (*Laughs.*) *Ein, zwei, drei!* (*Takes the cap off Firs and puts it on herself.*) When I was a little girl, my father and momma used to go from fairground to fairground, giving performances, pretty good ones. And I would be dressed as a boy and do the death-defying leap and all sorts of stunts, and so forth. And when Poppa and Momma died, a German gentlewoman took me home with her and started teaching me. Fine. I grew up, then turned into a governess. But where I'm from and who I am—I don't know . . . Who my parents were, maybe they weren't married . . . I don't know. (*Pulls a pickle from her pocket and eats it.*) I don't know anything.

FIRS. I was twenty or twenty-five, we're goin' along, me and the deacon's son and Vasily the cook, and there's this here man sittin' on a stone . . . a stranger like, don't know 'im . . . Somehow I git skeered and clear off, and when I'm gone they up and killed him . . . There was money on him.

[173]

CHARLOTTA. Well? *Weiter.*

FIRS. Then, I mean, comes a trial, they start askin' questions . . . They convict 'em . . . And me too . . . I sit in the penal colony two years or so . . . Then nothing, they let me go . . . A long time ago this was.

Pause.

You can't rec'llect all of it . . .

CHARLOTTA. It's time for you to die, Granddad. (*Eats the pickle.*)

FIRS. Huh? (*Mutters to himself.*) And then, I mean, we're all riding together, and there's a rest stop . . . Uncle leaped out of the wagon . . . took a sack . . . and in that sack's another sack. And he looks, and there's something in there — jerk! jerk!

CHARLOTTA (*laughs, quietly*). Jerk, jerk! (*Eats the pickle.*)

We hear someone quickly walking along the
road, playing a balalaika . . . The moon comes
up . . . Somewhere near the poplars VARYA is looking
for Anya and calling, "Anya! Where are you!"

Curtain (A1 & 2)

ACT THREE

page 129 / *After: "liking you very much, too."*

How are you?

Voice: "O, when I seen you, my heart got very sore." (A)